# The Beave

Daniel Farson lead[s] [you into the myster]ious world of the [horror. Read all] about ghosts and g[houls, vampires and were]wolves and monsters of all kinds, and meet your favourite horror characters. Frankenstein's Monster, Count Dracula and Jekyll and Hyde are all here, as well as many others from real life and fiction. You can find out about horror stories and their writers, horror films and actors and horror spots of the world, and see how much you know about horror by trying the exciting Quiz.

Daniel Farson is the son of the American writer Negley Farson and great-nephew of Bram Stoker, author of *Dracula*. A former journalist and T.V. personality, he is now a full-time writer of non-fiction and plays and an authority on the case of Jack the Ripper.

# The Beaver Book of HORROR

Daniel Farson

Beaver Books

First published in 1977 by
The Hamlyn Publishing Group Limited
London · New York · Sydney · Toronto
Astronaut House, Feltham, Middlesex, England
Reprinted 1977

© Copyright Text Daniel Farson 1977
ISBN 0 600 31395 6

Printed in England by
Hazell Watson & Viney Limited
Aylesbury, Bucks
Set in Monotype Bembo

For Peter Underwood,
President of the Ghost Club,
maestro of the occult and friend

All rights reserved. This book is sold subject to the
condition that it shall not in any manner be lent,
re-sold, hired or otherwise circulated without the
publisher's prior consent in writing in any form of
binding or cover other than that in which it is
published and without a similar condition including
this condition being imposed on the subsequent
purchaser. No part of the book may be reproduced,
stored in a retrieval system, or transmitted, in any
form or by any electronic, mechanical, photocopying
or recording means, or otherwise, without the
publisher's prior consent in writing.

# Contents

    **A Word of Warning**    9

    **A Horror Quiz**    10

1 **Of Ghosts and Ghouls**
    Things that go 'bump' in the night    14
    Time out of joint    16
    The pilot who saw the future    18
    Man with a coffin    20
    The sailors with the animal heads    22
    The curse of the stolen sacrum    24
    The Egyptian mummy    29
    An English 'daddy'    32

2 **Vampires**
    Are there such things?    34
    The land beyond the forest    35
    The British vampire    38
    Vampires today    39
    Simple explanations    41
    The man in Stoke-on-Trent    45

3 **Werewolves**
    The legend of the werewolf    48
    The case of Jean Grenier    53
    The beggar werewolf    55
    The werewolves of St Claude    55
    The German werewolf    56
    The werewolf and the sea captain    56
    Saved by a werewolf!    57
    What are they really?    59

## 4 Horror Stories

| | |
|---|---|
| Classic horror stories | 62 |
| Frankenstein | 64 |
| The Hunchback of Notre Dame | 70 |
| Seeing double | 72 |
| Edgar Allan Poe's 'tales' | 74 |
| The Strange Case of Dr Jekyll and Mr Hyde | 80 |
| The Picture of Dorian Gray | 90 |
| Dracula | 90 |
| The Phantom of the Opera | 99 |
| Sheridan Le Fanu | 101 |
| Ambrose Bierce | 103 |
| M. R. James | 105 |

## 5 Horror on Stage and Screen

| | |
|---|---|
| Curtains for Dracula | 108 |
| Horror film classics | 114 |
| Lon Chaney | 117 |
| Bela Lugosi | 119 |
| Boris Karloff | 121 |
| Christopher Lee | 126 |
| The future of the horror film | 129 |

## 6 Almost Human

| | |
|---|---|
| The Elephant Man | 132 |
| Wolf children | 138 |
| The leopard men | 144 |
| The vampire bat | 145 |
| The Black Dog of Death | 147 |
| The Nuckelavee | 150 |
| The Lambton Worm | 151 |
| The Island of Dr Moreau | 152 |

| | |
|---|---|
| The White Worm | 155 |
| The Black Cat | 158 |

## 7 Your Guide to Horror

| | |
|---|---|
| Haiti – home of the Zombie | 164 |
| The Place of Dread | 168 |
| The horror of Glamis | 171 |
| Whitby | 173 |
| Transylvania | 175 |
| Borley Rectory | 178 |
| Highgate cemetery, London | 181 |

## 8 Real Horrors

| | |
|---|---|
| Countess Bathory | 186 |
| Gilles de Rais | 186 |
| Dracula – Prince Vlad V of Wallachia | 187 |
| Ivan the Terrible | 188 |
| Rasputin | 189 |
| Sawney Bean, the Scottish cannibal | 191 |
| The Stranglers of Bombay | 193 |
| Jack the Ripper | 196 |
| The Vampire killer | 201 |

| | |
|---|---|
| **Answers to the Horror Quiz** | 203 |
| **Acknowledgements** | 206 |

# A WORD OF WARNING

To one person a snake is horrible, to another a spider – but just think, as they slide and scuttle away, how horrible we must seem to them!
Nothing is more horrifying than a sudden shadow at midnight, yet a heartbeat later you realise it was only a trick of moonlight.
So if some of these tales strike you as too horrible to bear, remember it is all in the mind.
The sad case of the Elephant Man proves how deceptive appearances can be.
The Black Dog of Death was probably a labrador.
Everything has an explanation.
Or has it?
Come to think of it, there are creatures that defy the imagination – werewolves, vampires, ghouls . . .
Perhaps it would be just as well to look under your bed before you turn out the light tonight.
Who knows *what* you will find!

*Daniel Farson*

# A HORROR QUIZ

1. In which city did a bone ruin a dinner party?
2. Who changed his mind and got out of a hotel lift?
3. Who broke his guest's shaving mirror?
4. Who was really a big white worm?
5. Which actor was buried wearing Dracula's cloak and ring?
6. Who married his thirteen-year-old cousin?
7. How did William Wilson die?
8. Who rewrote what book in the light of his wife's criticism?
9. Who died when the lights went out in Cairo?
10. Which star of silent films was known as 'The Man of a Thousand Faces'?
11. Name the doctor who tried to turn animals into human beings.
12. Whose mother told him stories about a cholera epidemic when he was ill in bed?
13. Name one object which scares off vampires.
14. Who was unjustly hanged for the murder of Frankenstein's brother?
15. What was unusual about Dorian Gray's picture?

## The Beaver Book of Horror

16  Who was in charge of make-up for the famous 1931 film of *Frankenstein*?
17  What was the name of the Phantom of the Opera?
18  What was the stage name of William Henry Pratt?
19  Where did the best-known British vampire live?
20  Who was evil – Jekyll or Hyde?
21  Did Count Dracula have a moustache?
22  Was Harry Price or Vincent Price a famous ghost hunter?
23  Which building has often been described as 'the most haunted house in England'?
24  Is Transylvania a real place?
25  What island is the traditional home of the Zombie?
26  On the shores of which lake was *Frankenstein* written?
27  What was the name of the Hunchback of Notre Dame?
28  What do hairs on the palms of your hands mean?
29  Who was known as 'The King of the Cannibal Islands'?
30  Who munched his lunch under a row of impaled bodies?

You will find the answers to all the questions in this book, and they are listed on page 203.

# 1
# OF GHOSTS AND GHOULS

*They are neither man nor woman –*
*They are neither brute nor human,*
*They are Ghouls.*

(*The Bells*
by Edgar Allan Poe)

## Things that go 'bump' in the night

> *'From ghoulies and ghosties and long-leggety beasties*
> *And things that go bump in the night,*
> *Good Lord, deliver us!'*
>
> (*A Scottish prayer*)

Ghosts are seen so often they are somehow easier to believe in than vampires, for instance. A ghost is a dead person who appears to a living one. Some people see a ghost, or think they do, while others around them see nothing at all. Sometimes there is nothing to see – just the sensation that some 'thing' is there, making the spine tingle and the fur of the dog rise up in horror:

> *'As I was going up the stair*
> *I met a man who wasn't there.*
> *He wasn't there again today.*
> *I wish, I wish he'd stay away.'*
>
> (*Hughes Mearns*)

The ghost or spectre is usually thought of as a white transparent shape bumping around at night, but can also be seen in the exact form of a human being and in daylight too. Sometimes he is a familiar figure seen in an ordinary place, like the old clergyman spotted by the American writer Nathaniel Hawthorne, sitting in a chair by the fireplace reading the *Boston Post* in the Atheneum Library. Hawthorne was astounded when he learnt that the old man had been dead for several weeks, but he continued to see him. Explaining later why he never tried to touch the ghost, he wrote: 'Perhaps I was loth to destroy the illusion, and to rob myself of so good a ghost story, which might probably

*Of Ghosts and Ghouls*

have been explained in some very commonplace way.' He admitted also that he was afraid of making a fool of himself by speaking to an empty chair in such a solemn place as the Atheneum, where all conversation was forbidden. And, as a final excuse, he added that they had 'never been introduced'. One day the old man disappeared, and Hawthorne never saw 'it' again.

Unlike vampires, who destroy people by biting them, the ghost is usually harmless. There are those who enjoy scaring people, like Marley's ghost clanking his chains in Charles Dickens' story *A Christmas Carol*, but there are also kindly ghosts who appear as a warning of approaching trouble, and help a person to avoid it.

Most of us have met someone who believes that he or she has seen a ghost. Even the author of this book saw one, and a very dull ghost it was too, which made it all the more convincing. In 1974 I was staying at Young's Hotel – an extremely old house opposite the vast cathedral in York known as the Minster. Waking suddenly in the middle of the night, I saw the figure of a short, rather round monk looking at me from the far corner of the room beside a wardrobe near the window. I reached forward to see if I could touch 'it', for I realised this was a ghost, but the figure disappeared. There was no question of a lingering dream, but when I told the owners of the hotel about this the next morning, wondering if there was some legend associated with the building, they laughed at me.

Ghosts are seen so often that it is tempting to believe in such beings, trapped in places they once knew, suspended in a state between life and death. This would explain why so many ghosts seem to be people who have died unnaturally, from suicide or murder, and who are searching for someone to help them find peace. In this sense the ghost is a 'lost soul'. One of the first ghosts to be recorded, a hundred years before the birth of Christ, is a case in point. The figure of an old man, his hands and feet bound in chains, was supposed to haunt a house in Athens, and after one person was frightened to death, the house was deserted. A philosopher called Athenodorous became curious when he heard the rumours and the low rent that was being asked for the house. He moved in to investigate. Sure enough, there was a clanking of chains and a figure appeared, beckoning him to follow. Athenodorous pretended not to see the spectre, who gave up and crossed the courtyard, still rattling his chains, and disappeared. But Athenodorous had noted the spot, and the following morning he sent for a magistrate to help him. When they dug up the corner in the courtyard, they found the remains of a skeleton bound in chains, and after the magistrate ordered a proper reburial the ghost was never seen again.

It is equally likely that the ghost is a memory conjured up by the living person – a projection of the living rather than the dead. This suggests a form of telepathy (one person transmitting a thought to another), though in this case the thought actually takes shape. Is this any more unbelievable than the theory of psychokinesis, by which objects can be moved by sheer concentration of thought alone rather than physical effort?

Even more fascinating is the possibility that time can slip out of place. A missed beat in time is one of the likeliest explanations for sightings of ghosts.

### Time out of joint

People sometimes experience the feeling 'I have been here before' about places, people and events. They get the impression that they have been in a particular place once before, or met a certain person at another moment in time, even though they know this is impossible. This feeling is called *déjà vu* – the French for 'already seen'. The opposite is possible too – glimpses into the future, as brief but as sensitive as the click of a camera. It is just conceivable (though this is only a far-out guess) that the Loch Ness Monster is a memory image of the past, while flying saucers are machines of the future!

There are many curious stories of lapses in time – one concerns an Irish priest who died in a remote part of the countryside. After his funeral, the mourners made their way back from the graveyard on the hill, and were startled to see the black figure of a priest coming towards them. As he passed, they recognised the man they had just buried. Deeply disturbed, they hurried to his home to find the dead man's mother in a state of shock – he had just appeared to her too.

Then there is the famous case of the two English ladies who found themselves lost in the gardens of Versailles near Paris, when they stumbled on a group of people dressed very finely in the sort of costumes worn several centuries earlier. When they described the scene afterwards, people recognised members of the French court of Louis XIV. Was this a time lapse? There have been suggestions that the women had interrupted a group of friends who had been 'dressing-up', but there have been many cases of past incidents being witnessed by people who could not have known them or been able to describe them otherwise.

This comes close to the mysterious world of dreams – is this where we have seen the place or person before? Not all that long ago, the native of Brazil or Guiana would be convinced that his soul was out hunting or fishing, or whatever he was dreaming about, while his body stayed motionless in his hammock. Primitive people were always careful not to wake someone who was asleep, because his soul was away and might not have time to return, and if a man wakes without his soul, he falls sick and dies. Soul – spirit – ghost – the borderlines are close.

As always, Shakespeare puts it best: 'Thou coms't in such a questionable shape,' Hamlet tells the ghost of his father, uncertain if he is a 'spirit of health, or goblin damned'.

## The pilot who saw the future

Frank Smyth, editor of *Man, Myth and Magic* and *Modern Witchcraft* (1971) and author of *Ghosts and Poltergeists* (1976) knows what he's talking about when it concerns the supernatural. The most impressive 'true' ghost story he has come across is the following, and the ghost is no transparent figure in a white nightie, but a wing-commander in the last war.

Wing-Commander George Potter was a squadron leader at an RAF base in Egypt, which sent out bombers to drop mines in the sea-routes of Rommel's supply ships. They operated at night and flew during a 'bomber's moon' – when the full moon reflected on the water helped them to navigate the Mediterranean. Between flights they tried to enjoy themselves, drinking, smoking and talking.

One evening Potter entered the mess with Flying Officer Reg Lamb for a nightcap, and looked around to see who else was there. He noticed another wing-commander, called Roy, who was surrounded by friends.

Potter and Lamb finished their drinks, when there was a burst of laughter from Roy's corner and Potter turned round:

'Then I saw it. I turned and saw the head and shoulders of the wing-commander moving ever so slowly in a bottomless depth of blue-blackness. His lips were drawn back from his teeth in a dreadful grin; he had eye-sockets but no eyes; the remaining flesh of his face was duly blotched in greenish, purplish shadows, with shreds peeling off near his left ear.

'I gazed. It seemed that my heart had swollen and stopped. I experienced all the storybook sensations of utter horror. The hair on my temples and the back of my neck felt like wire, icy sweat trickled down my spine, and I trembled slightly all over. I was vaguely aware of faces nearby, but the horrible death mask dominated the lot.'

Gradually he realised that Flying Officer Lamb was tugging at his sleeve.

'What the hell's the matter?' he asked. 'You've gone as white as a sheet . . . as if you've seen a ghost!'

'I *have* seen a ghost,' said Potter. 'Roy has the mark of death on him.'

Lamb looked over, but Roy seemed perfectly normal to him. But Potter was still shocked, especially as he knew that Roy would be flying the following night. He wondered if he should go to the group captain with such a story, in the hope that Roy would be grounded, but decided against such an action. He said later, 'I am convinced that the decision not to interfere was part of a preordained sequence of events.'

He waited for news throughout the next night. At dawn the telephone rang with the news that Roy and his crew had been shot down, but the plane had ditched safely and the crew had been spotted clambering into a life raft. Potter felt an enormous sense of relief, but it was short-lived. Though they searched for them afterwards, Roy and his crew were never seen again. Then Potter knew what he had seen: '... the blue-black nothingness was the Mediterranean Sea at night, and he was floating somewhere in it, dead...'

Frank Smyth concludes the story: 'The vivid accurate details of the terrible vision suggest that Potter had, for a moment, been able to look into the future.'

## Man with a coffin

This story has been collected by Peter Underwood, President of the Ghost Club, and is the basis for many similar ghost stories. The episode took place in 1890 in an Irish country house called Tullamore, not far from the sea port of Wexford. It concerns Lord Dufferin, a distinguished man and a former Viceroy of India. Not the man to be scared of ghosts, he was a soldier, cool and self-possessed. His grandson stated later: 'The story is perfectly true, but my grandfather could never explain it ... because he did not believe in ghosts.'

After spending an enjoyable evening at a friend's house-party in Tullamore, Lord Dufferin went up to his bedroom. He felt at peace with the world, there was a comforting wood fire in the grate and he decided to read a little before going to sleep. After half an hour, he felt curiously restless and put the book down. Then he dozed fitfully.

Usually Lord Dufferin slept well, but at two o'clock he got out of bed and crossed to the window. It was a cloudless night with a full moon (always a full moon in such stories!) and everything was still. Then, suddenly, something caught his eye and he watched fascinated as a figure stepped out from the shadows and walked slowly across the lawn carrying a large box on his back. He stopped when he was opposite the bedroom window and stared up at

Lord Dufferin. The moon lit the man's face – their eyes met – Lord Dufferin moved back instinctively. He described the man's face later as 'full of horror and malevolence'. As the man turned away and disappeared, Lord Dufferin realised that the box he was carrying was a coffin. The house was as quiet as death and he returned to bed.

When he came down to breakfast the next morning, Lord Dufferin told everyone about his adventure. They had a good laugh and his friend assured him that the house had no history of a ghost. Sure enough, on further visits Lord Dufferin slept in the same bedroom and nothing happened.

And that was all? No. Years later, when he had been appointed Ambassador to France, Lord Dufferin waited at the lift of a Paris hotel where he was going to address a conference on the Fifth Floor. The lift came down, the doors opened, people came out and others went in, including Lord Dufferin, who was busy in conversation. Suddenly he looked up and noticed the liftman. He stepped back appalled. It was the face he had seen in Ireland, the face of the man who carried the coffin on his back. He waved the lift away and the doors closed.

A few moments later, as it reached the Fifth Floor, there was a sharp noise followed by a dreadful crash which shook the hotel. The suspension cable had snapped and the lift had plunged to the bottom of the shaft, killing five of the people in it, including the liftman.

Who was the liftman? Lord Dufferin wanted to know, but, curiously enough, no one could tell him. He had replaced the regular liftman only that morning. The hotel had no idea who he was and never discovered where he came from. Yet, by some strange trick of time, he had saved Lord Dufferin's life.

## The sailors with the animal heads

One of the most extraordinary, though little known, Irish ghost stories unearthed by Peter Underwood took place in a small house beside the River Suir in County Waterford.

Appropriately it happened at midnight on Christmas Eve. Eli Hayson was going to bed when he was disturbed by the noise of running footsteps along the waterfront outside. Looking out of the window on to the moonlit quay, he saw a young man in grey jersey and dark trousers running desperately towards the house.

As he came closer, Eli recognised his twin brother Jack, a sailor who was supposed to be on a ship called the *Thomas Emery* at Cork. He was about to go down and open the door when he noticed several figures following his brother – strangely, they seemed to rise out of the water. He tried to shout a warning but found he could not move and could not speak. His brother reached the door and tried to open it, but the dark figures closed in around him. For a moment Eli saw his brother's face convulsed with fear, and heard the single cry: 'For God's sake, help me!'

At that moment the moon was hidden by a cloud. When it reappeared, everything was peaceful and Eli was able to move at last. He hurried to the door, but as there was no sign of his brother Jack or anyone else he decided he must have had a bad dream.

Two days later, the captain of the *Thomas Emery* sent the bad news – Jack had fallen overboard and drowned. Apparently he had been sleep-walking. At the inquest in Cork, Jack's father testified he had never known his sons to walk in their sleep, but members of the crew swore they had seen Jack leave his bunk and walk around the ship at night. A verdict of 'Found Drowned' was returned, though the family refused to believe the story.

## Of Ghosts and Ghouls

Many years later, Eli was drinking in his favourite pub in Cork when the landlord told him that an old man who lived in the town might be able to tell him something of interest. He finished his drink and walked to the address he had been given, where he found an old man called Matthew Webster. When he learned Eli's name he was reluctant to talk, but at last he revealed the secret that his son Tom had told him shortly before his death two months earlier. It concerned an incident witnessed twenty years before, on a Christmas Eve. Tom had been warming himself by a fire on the quayside when he heard footsteps. Looking up he saw three horrifying figures walking stealthily along the water's edge, They had the bodies of men in sailors' clothes, but their heads were those of animals – apes and stags.

Though he was terrified, he was curious too and crept after them. They went down some steps and rowed off in a dinghy, boarding a schooner moored in the harbour. Tom took another boat and followed, climbing up to the stern of the ship where he hid among some barrels.

His blood turned cold when, from his hiding place, he heard loud groans and shrieks of terror. Suddenly a young man leapt out of the companionway and raced across the deck, pursued by the sinister men with the animal heads.

It was a moonlit night and Tom could see the fear on the young man's face as he ran past, screaming 'For God's sake, help me!' Tom rushed forward impulsively, but the young man jumped overboard. He was about to dive in after him when the creatures seized him. It was now that Tom discovered they were not a figment of his imagination, but real men wearing masks. It was all an elaborate plot by three members of the crew to frighten the young man to death – and they succeeded. Two of them wanted to kill Tom also, but the third was prepared to spare him if he promised to keep quiet. Listening to their threats of what would happened if he breathed a word of what he had seen, Tom swore a solemn oath to say nothing. But the young man's face haunted him, and he told his father about the incident when he was dying.

Eli asked the old man if he knew the date when this happened. Matthew Webster took a pocket book from a chest of drawers – needless to say, the date was the same as the Christmas Eve when Eli 'saw' his brother Jack at the door of their house.

Ghosts are frequently seen by a close relative at the moment of death, and there is a particular affinity between identical twins. A few years ago a newspaper reported the true case of one twin dying at sea and his brother, thousands of kilometres away, dying at the same moment on land – a moment of acute stress shared by someone exceptionally close. At the moment of Jack's death, pursued by his enemies, it seems quite possible that his twin brother would have felt and seen something.

### The curse of the stolen sacrum

Peter Underwood, to whom this book is dedicated, believes he has heard more true ghost stories than any man alive. He considers the following to be the most convincing ghost story of all, and this account is based on his version.

In 1936, Sir Alexander Seton, 10th Baronet of Abercorn and armour-bearer to the Queen, set sail for Egypt with his wife Zayla. They visited the usual places – the Temple at Luxor and the tomb of Tutankhamun. When their guide showed them around the Great Pyramid, he told them of a tomb that was being excavated nearby and offered to take them there. After making their way down thirty rough stone steps, they entered a room where a

## Of Ghosts and Ghouls

crumbling female skeleton was laid out on a stone slab.

Back in their hotel that night, Lady Seton showed her husband a bone she had taken away with her when she slipped back, unnoticed, for a final look. 'It looked like a digestive biscuit,' wrote Sir Alexander. In fact it was the sacrum, a triangular bone connecting the base of the spine with the pelvis.

Safely home in Edinburgh, the Setons told their friends of their journey and showed them the bone which Sir Alexander kept in a glass case on a corner table in the dining-room. Strange incidents then began to occur – so strange that Sir Alexander began to wonder if he was under a curse for possessing the stolen sacrum. As his guests left the house, a huge piece of the roof came crashing down within a metre of him. The next morning a chimney blew off, but as there was a strong wind at the time Sir Alexander did not take this too seriously. However, a few nights later, the children's nanny burst into his bedroom to say she heard someone moving about in the dining-room below. When he went down everything seemed all right, though he thought he heard a crash later on. Finding the corner table overturned the next morning, with the glass case on the floor, his wife was sure he must have upset it in the night without realising it. Sir Alexander knew he had not, but thought it could have overturned because of the vibration from traffic outside.

From then on, all sorts of curious things were heard and seen. A nephew saw 'a funny-dressed person going down the stairs', servants were alarmed by a 'spectral robed figure wandering about the house at night', and some of them gave notice and left. By now, Sir Alexander was alarmed too. He took the sacrum to the drawing-room upstairs, locked the doors and windows, and kept watch outside on the balcony. Nothing happened, so after waiting there several hours he went to bed. Almost at once, so it seemed, his wife woke him up shouting that someone was moving about in the drawing-room. Seizing his revolver, he met the nanny in the passage, also woken by the noises. Unlocking the door, he found the room had been broken into – '... it looked as if a battle royal had taken place' – with chairs and books thrown all over the place. The Egyptian bone, however, remained where he had put it.

Sir Alexander checked the windows, but there was no way anyone could have entered. A short period of comparative peace followed, apart from two mysterious fires and the bangs and crashes the family was now used to. However, all too soon the room was disturbed again, more violently this time, with ornaments broken and glass smashed, and '... even the table on which the Bone stood seemed to have been subjected to some kind of severe pressure for one leg was cracked.'

A Scottish newspaper heard of the story and published the headline:

BARONET FEARS PHARAOH CURSE ON FAMILY

One of the reporters borrowed the Bone for a few days, but nothing happened. Two weeks later he collapsed and had to have an emergency operation.

Shortly after the Bone was returned to the Setons' drawing-room, the nanny heard another tremendous crash – it was found on the floor, broken into five pieces. Various suggestions were made: that Lady Seton should return to Egypt and replace the Bone in the tomb (she wouldn't hear of it), or that it should be buried or thrown into the sea. Sir Alexander refused to sell the thing, afraid of what might happen to anyone who bought it.

## Of Ghosts and Ghouls

Meanwhile, Lady Seton had taken the sacrum to a doctor, who put the pieces together, and it was restored to the house and placed on a table in the hall. One evening, during a dinner party, both the table and the Bone were hurled across the hall, striking the dining-room wall with such violence that the maid fainted, a cousin swooned, the guests became hysterical and the dinner was spoilt. It was time to get rid of the Bone. While his wife was away, Sir Alexander asked his uncle, Father Benedict of the Abbey at Fort Augustus, to perform an exorcism. The Bone was blessed, then it was burnt until no trace of it was left.

Did the Bone carry a curse? Sir Alexander believed the Egyptian sacrum was responsible for many of his later misfortunes. His daughter, who was five at the time, remembers the Bone as 'an evil thing', and claims: 'I always believed that there was something in the curse.'

The Seton case makes a particularly interesting ghost (or poltergeist) story, because it raises the whole subject of Egyptian curses. The Mummy's Curse was originally made by priests of ancient Egypt, who performed magical rites to make certain that no one disturbed the tombs of their dead rulers.

Such a curse was a useful warning to scare off robbers, but it was gradually noticed that when a tomb was opened unusual things often happened to those responsible.

At two in the morning, on 5th April, 1923, the lights went out in Cairo, the capital of Egypt. At exactly the same moment, the fifth Earl of Caernarvon died in his Cairo hotel. The reason for the blackout was given as a power failure, though it was described by the chief engineer as 'scientifically impossible'. In England, that same evening, the Earl's dog howled and moaned in the Caernarvon country home until it fell dead at the same moment as its master. Was this yet another example of apparent thought transference at the moment of death, or was it something more?

The Earl had led the recent expedition to Egypt which unearthed the golden treasure house of the boy-king Tutankhamun who died around 1350 B.C. It was one of the greatest archaeological finds in history. During the diggings the Earl was bitten by a mosquito, and later the bite became swollen and infected. Perhaps this was the reason for his death, but the explanation is not entirely satisfactory.

There *is* something strange about the Pyramids. As recently as 1969, a physicist in charge of experiments concerning the measurements of the Pyramids told a correspondent of the *Times* newspaper: 'Either the geometry of the pyramid is in substantial error ... or there is a mystery which is beyond explanation – call it what you will, occultism, the curse of the Pharaohs, sorcery or magic – there is some force that defies the laws of sciences at work in the pyramid.'

The shape of the Pyramids appears to possess a power of its own. In his book *Supernature*, Lyall Watson reported the experiment of leaving a blunt razor blade inside a cardboard model of the Great Pyramid of Cheops, and finding it sharp in the morning! He concluded that even the replica had 'special properties'. A Frenchman, Monsieur Bovis, had already discovered that bodies of small animals left in the burial chamber of the Pharaoh Cheops did not decay as they should have done. There seemed a natural process of mummification. As the chamber was situated in the centre of the Pyramid, a third of the way from the base to the apex, it seemed that there was a relation between the shape and size of the structure and the chemical processes going on inside. Perhaps this fact helped the Egyptians when they mummified their rulers. It is a fascinating theme. As with so many aspects of the supernatural, why shouldn't there be powers of which we have no idea? The exciting thing is that we seem on the verge of understanding so much – for example Colin Wilson, the ghost expert, believes that ghosts will become explicable within the next hundred years.

## The Egyptian mummy

In his book *Haunted London*, Peter Underwood tells the story of the mummy case of a high priestess which ended up in London. He claims: 'It does seem indisputable that from the time the mummy case passed into the possession of an Englishman in Egypt about 1860 a strange series of fatalities followed its journey and even when it resided in the Mummy Room at the British Museum sudden death haunted those who handled the 3500-year-old relic from Luxor.'

A palmist called Cheiro read the hand of a young man called Douglas Murray, and felt an immediate dread that the man's right arm would be damaged after touching some sacred prize, and that a series of misfortunes would follow. A few years later Murray returned to England, an empty sleeve fastened across his chest. While in Egypt an Arab had shown him the magnificent mummy case of a high priestess of the Temple of Amen-Ra, whose face was immortalised on the outside in gold and enamel. Douglas Murray bought the mummy case and arranged for its shipment back to England. A few days later, while duck-shooting on the Nile, his shotgun exploded. It shattered his right arm, which became infected with gangrene and had to be amputated.

Back in London Murray found the mummy waiting in his hallway. Something very odd had happened to it! The face that had looked so young and beautiful now seemed old and incredibly evil. When a journalist asked to borrow the mummy case, he agreed readily. As soon as it entered her house, all sorts of calamities followed – her mother fell downstairs and died, her pedigree dogs went mad and her 'young man' broke off their engagement. She gave the mummy back to Murray but he didn't want it, which is not altogether surprising. He presented it to the British Museum and asked a friend to arrange its transfer. Within weeks the friend was dead and his servant testified that his master had been unable to sleep while the mummy stayed in the house waiting to be moved.

Was it safe in the British Museum at last? Well, the carrier who brought it there died a week later, and it was noticed (though it must have been coincidence) that unfortunate things seemed to happen to anyone who took too great an interest in the mummy. It has been claimed that the British Museum, thankful to be rid of it, presented the mummy case with apparent generosity to a museum in New York and shipped it across the Atlantic. And the name of the ship which carried it? The 'unsinkable' *Titanic*, which sank.

It is tempting to dismiss such stories, except that many distinguished people believe in them. The ghost hunter Thurston Hopkins claimed that thirteen people who handled the mummy case met death or disaster, including a photographer who found another woman's face in the print he had taken, and then went home and shot himself because it was 'so horrid and frightening'. Hopkins told Peter Underwood that he had spoken to a keeper in the Mummy Room of the British Museum who had seen a

## Of Ghosts and Ghouls

'figure' suddenly sit up in the empty bottom half of the mummy case. Then 'something with a horrible yellow face glided towards him with a sickeningly smooth movement, until he thought he was going to be pushed down a trapdoor.' He leapt up but his hands met nothing and the figure disappeared.

It is just possible that Bram Stoker, author of *Dracula*, knew this story. In 1910 he published a sensational novel, *Jewel of Seven Stars*, about an eminent Egyptologist called Abel Trelawney who has taken the mummy of an Egyptian Queen, Tara, to his house in London. All sorts of disasters follow – at one point he is found by his bedside bleeding from a wrist wound of seven parallel scratches. However, he is determined to attempt the impossible and bring the mummy back to life. Nothing will dissuade him. The story, next to *Dracula* in suspense and readability, reaches a grand climax:

> 'The storm still thundered around the house, and I could feel the rock on which it was built tremble under the furious onslaught of the waves. The shutters strained as though the screaming wind without would in very anger have forced an entrance. In that dread hour of expectancy, when the forces of Life and Death were struggling for the mastery, imagination was awake. I almost fancied that the storm was a living thing and animated with the wrath of the quick!
> 
> 'All at once the eager faces round the sarcophagus were bent forward. The look of speechless wonder in the eyes, lit by that supernatural glow from within the sarcophagus, had a more than mortal brilliance. My own eyes were nearly blinded by the awful paralysing light, so that I could hardly trust them. I saw

something white rising from the open sarcophagus...
something which appeared to my tortured eyes to
be filmy, like a white mist. In the heart of this mist,
which was cloudy and opaque like an opal, was something like a hand holding a fiery jewel flaming with
many lights, As the fierce glow of the Coffer met this
new living light, the green vapour floating between
them seemed like a cascade of brilliant points, a miracle of light!'

Then all hell breaks loose! The storm bursts through the shutters and destroys the bold yet sacrilegious experiment, which ends in horror.

### An English 'daddy'

After all this talk of Egyptian mummies, let's finish with an English 'daddy'.

The mummified remains of Jeremy Bentham (1748–1832) are preserved in a glass case in the entrance to University College, London. There he sits, fully dressed and as large as life. Bentham was a law reformer, scientist and eccentric who wanted his body preserved after his death so that 'he' could attend meetings of his admirers. He was obsessed with the subject of mummification, and even toyed with the idea of mummifying people's ancestors so that they could provide permanent memorials – rows of dead people lining the drives of stately homes! He discussed the treatment of his own body before his death, but his head decayed too rapidly and was replaced by a wax model. Even so, the lifelike figure sitting there with favourite cane, white gloves and hat is horrible enough. Bentham's ghost is supposed to haunt the college at night, tap-tapping along the corridors. A former maths master saw it plainly, but it passed through him and disappeared.

# 2
# VAMPIRES

*'Rubbish Watson, rubbish! What have we to do with walking corpses who can only be held in their graves by stakes driven through their hearts? It's pure lunacy.'*

(The Adventures of the Sussex Vampire
by Sir Arthur Conan Doyle)

**Are there such things?**

At the end of his stage production of *Dracula*, Hamilton Deane stepped in front of the curtain and addressed the audience:

> 'Just a moment, ladies and gentlemen! Just a word before you leave. We hope the memories of Dracula and Renfield won't give you bad dreams, so just a word of reassurance. When you get home tonight, and the lights have been turned out, and you are afraid to look behind the curtains, and you dread to see a face appear at the window, why, just pull yourself together and remember that after all – THERE ARE SUCH THINGS!'

A vampire is someone who is between life and death. Count Dracula was described as one of the 'undead'. A vampire is the creature of the night. When the sun sets he becomes active, and after climbing out of his coffin he assumes the shape of a live person. But at the first sign of daylight he has to return to his coffin, where he lies motionless, as if dead.

Anyone, male or female, is in danger of becoming a vampire once bitten, for this is how the vampire survives – by sucking the blood of the living. So the idea of the vampire as a thin, white-faced creature is wrong. On the contrary, after a feast of blood the vampire will be fat and rosy-cheeked.

How do you recognise a vampire? There are so many theories that almost anyone can be mistaken for a vampire – those born on Christmas Day, seventh sons of seventh sons, anyone with eyebrows that join, red hair or blue eyes – all are suspect! This is fantasy of course, but if you meet someone who has no reflection or shadow, then you should be worried – vampires cannot be seen in glass and cast no shadow.

How can you protect yourself? Remember that the vampire is terrified by two things – garlic and a crucifix or anything in the shape of a cross. How do you destroy a vampire? First catch him, preferably when he is lying inside his coffin. Then it is necessary to hammer a wooden stake straight through his heart with a single blow. If you find this too horrific (and who can blame you?) then remember that the vampire can also be destroyed by the light of day. If you meet him after dawn, open the curtains or force him into the sunlight and he will turn to dust. If he has become a wolf, he can only be killed by a silver bullet.

So, do vampires really exist? On the face of it, few beliefs could be sillier – that dead people should rise from their graves at night to suck the blood of the living – yet people have believed in vampires since the beginning of time.

### The land beyond the forest

The true stamping ground – or gliding ground – of the vampire is Eastern Europe – Austria, Hungary, Yugoslavia and Romania. Romania was split into three states until the First World War – Wallachia, Moldovia and Transylvania.

A clergyman called Montague Summers, one of the most famous experts on the history of the vampire, has written '... in Romania we find gathered together around the Vampire almost all the beliefs and superstitions that prevail throughout the whole of Eastern Europe.'

He mentions superstition – is this all there was to it? Certainly this is just what we should expect in remote parts of the 'land beyond the forest', infested by wolves, where people were darkly ignorant. It's hardly surprising if they were superstitious. A typical story is that of the young soldier returning home from war, who meets a girl as he walks beside the lake close to his village. She is pale, dark-haired and beautiful. They talk, and suddenly he notices that though he can see his own reflection in the water there is no one beside him. He falls, fainting, and when he recovers he really is alone. Arriving home he tells everyone of his meeting with the girl, only to be greeted with cries of horror – she has died several weeks earlier.

Some cases of vampirism have been officially witnessed and recorded by magistrates, priests and army officers, who should have known better than to believe in 'old wives' tales'. In 1732 a deputation was sent from Belgrade to investigate the report of a vampire who was attacking a family in a remote village in Yugoslavia. They were distinguished men – civil and military officials, a Public Prosecutor, various 'respected persons', twenty-four soldiers and a lieutenant of the Prince of Wurtemberg. They discovered that a man who had died three years before had returned as a vampire and killed three of his nieces and nephews and one brother in the last fortnight. He had started to suck the blood of his fifth victim, a beautiful young niece, when he was interrupted and escaped.

As darkness fell the deputation went to the man's grave, followed by a crowd of frightened villagers. When they opened his coffin he looked as healthy as anyone there – his hair, fingernails, teeth, and even his eyes (which were half-open) were all intact. One detail of this story is mentioned casually, but is sensational – the man's heart was still beating. When they pierced it with an iron bar, a white fluid burst out, mixed with blood Then they cut off his head with an axe and buried his body in quicklime, after which the last girl who had been attacked began to recover.

Another famous case was recorded by Dom Calmet, a leading historian on the subject. This concerned a Hungarian soldier who was billeted with a family. One night at supper he noticed a stranger join them at table and thought the whole family seemed curiously frightened. The next morning the soldier was told that the head of the family was dead and that the stranger was his father who had died ten years earlier. Alarmed by all this, the soldier reported the incident to his commanding officer, and the family were questioned by the authorities, including an army surgeon. The story was repeated and when the father was dug up from his grave he looked like a man who had just died – 'his blood like that of a living man'. The Captain of the Regiment, a Count de Cabrenas, ordered the vampire's head to be cut off.

An interesting example of how one vampire can infect another was reported to the Imperial Council of War in Vienna in the 1730s, when there seems to have been an epidemic of vampirism in Central Europe. It concerned another soldier, a Hungarian called Arnold Paul or Paole.

Paul was killed when a cart turned over on top of him, but it was claimed that he returned from the dead a month later and attacked four people who died from loss of blood – the fate traditionally reserved for victims of vampires.

Some friends remembered that Paul said he had been attacked by a vampire himself when he was doing his military service on the Turko-Serbian border. Believing in the old superstition, that victims become vampires themselves after death, he had used the traditional remedy of eating earth from the vampire's grave and rubbing himself with its blood, and thought he was cured. But these precautions failed, for when his body was dug up following the attacks, it showed all the signs of an arch-vampire: 'His body was flushed; his hair, nails and beard had grown, and his veins were full of liquid blood...'

The local Governor, who knew the 'drill', ordered the usual stake to be thrust through the heart, and the vampire uttered the familiar shriek. Then the people burnt his body and, to make absolutely sure, did the same things to the four people he had killed. And that, they thought, was that. But they overlooked one thing – Arnold Paul had attacked animals as well as human beings.

Five years later there was another outbreak of vampirism in the same village and seventeen people died. A woman woke screaming in the night saying that her son, Milo, who had died nine weeks earlier, had tried to strangle her. When she died three days later, Milo's body was dug up and found to be that of a vampire. When the Governor ordered another inquiry, it was discovered that all the 'new vampires' had eaten flesh from the same animals that had been attacked by Arnold Paul. This time they took no risks – the bodies were staked, beheaded and burned. For good luck the ashes were thrown into the river and swept away. This ended the terror forever.

## The British vampire

The best-known British vampire lived in Cumberland at Croglin Grange, according to the story told by a Captain Fisher to the writer Augustus Hare. No one seems to know of a Croglin Grange today, but there is a farmhouse called Croglin Lower Hall, not far from the churchyard, and Croglin can be found on the map. It means 'crooked river' – a perfect description for Croglin Water, which flows round Watch Hill.

Captain Fisher said the Grange, which overlooked the nearby church, was rented by two brothers and their young sister. One night as the girl lay in bed she glimpsed something moving across the lawn in the moonlight. A few moments later she was horrified to hear the sound of scratching at her window, and then she saw a brown figure with flaming eyes behind the glass. With long, bone-like fingers 'it' tried to unpick the lead, while she watched, too frightened to move. When a pane fell out 'it' reached inside and unlocked the window. The creature dragged the girl's head over the bed and sank its teeth into her throat as she started to scream. Her brothers came running when they heard the noise, to find their sister unconscious and bleeding while the creature escaped.

In order to recover from the shock, they took the girl to Switzerland for a holiday. When they returned to the house, at her insistence, everything seemed peaceful enough, but one winter's night she heard that terrible 'scratch, scratch, scratch' on her window again. As she saw the same 'hideous brown face' she screamed, and this time her brothers saw the creature scrambling across the lawn, and fired, shooting 'it' in the leg. The next day they followed a trail of blood to a family vault in the churchyard, and discovered that all the coffins except one had been broken into. When this was opened, they saw 'it' – brown and mummified, the same hideous face that had looked through the window, with a bullet in its leg.

### Vampires today

The idea of vampires is hard to accept even in darkest Transylvania in the middle of the eighteenth century, so it seems incredible that they should be 'alive' and biting now.

Yet there are some startling 'cases', even in the twentieth

century. For example, take the case of a girl called Lillith from New York. She told two psychic researchers that she had gone to a cemetery, where a young man tried to kiss her. It is not too clear what she was doing there, but suddenly she became possessed by a surge of strength and plunged her teeth into the man's neck, drawing blood. 'I never considered myself a Dracula,' she said, 'but rather a very evil person who like a taste of blood.'

In 1974 a gypsy woman in Romania, called Tinka, recalled her father's death when she was a girl. His body was laid out in the traditional way, but when the family tried to lift his legs to fit him in the burial clothes, they discovered that 'rigor mortis' had not set in and his limbs were soft. In fact 'rigor mortis' is only a temporary state, but they were so horrified that the story spread rapidly through the village – they had a vampire in their midst!

So what did they do? Perhaps you can guess – the villagers marched to the house, tore off the sheet that covered the corpse, and plunged a wooden stake through the man's heart.

Even in London, as recently as 1975, two cases of vampirism were reported by the Reverend Christopher Neil-Smith, a well-known exorcist who lives at St Saviour's Vicarage in Eton Road, Hampstead. He is convinced that vampirism is possible, because of the cases that have been brought to him: 'The one that particularly strikes me is that of a woman who showed me the marks on her wrists which appeared at night, where blood had definitely been taken. And there was no apparent reason why this should have occurred. They were marks almost like those of an animal. Something like scratching.'

The Reverend Neil-Smith does not believe this was done by the woman herself, who came to him when she felt her blood was being drained away. After he performed the exorcism the marks disappeared.

A man who came from South America 'had a similar phenomenon, as if an animal had sucked away his blood and attacked him at night.' Neil-Smith makes it plain that this man was intelligent enough to recognise the abnormal: 'He thought he had been attacked by a vampire. I must admit I was a bit suspicious at that time, I'll be quite honest. Then when he showed evidence I came to realise this was obviously correct.'

Most people will refuse to recognise these as genuine cases of vampirism, but rather the fantasies of a vivid imagination. The Reverend Neil-Smith disagrees: 'I think that's a very naïve interpretation. All the evidence points to the contrary.'

## Simple explanations

Without wishing to pour cold water (or garlic juice!) on the idea of the vampire, there are a number of simple reasons which explain the legend. Dennis Wheatley, author of such thrillers as *The Devil Rides Out*, has a convincing theory that in times of extreme poverty beggars would make their homes in graveyards, emerging from tombs in the cover of darkness to scavenge for food. If they were seen in the moonlight, stealing out of coffins, it is not surprising that rumours spread quickly by word of mouth.

There is another obvious theory which explains a great deal – that vampires were really unfortunate people who had been buried alive. Premature burial has taken place on occasions right up to the present day, for the simple reason that a state of death is extremely difficult to certify. In 1885, the *British Medical Journal* stated: 'It is true that hardly any one sign of death, short of putrefaction, can be relied on as infallible.' This is just as true today – only when the body starts to decay can you be absolutely certain.

A number of Victorians were terrified of being buried alive. Wilkie Collins, who wrote two of the first and most famous thrillers – *The Moonstone* and *The Woman in White* – left instructions for various tests to be made before he was buried, so that there should be no doubt that he was dead. A Russian, Count Karnicki, invented a coffin with a glass ball resting on top of the body. If the corpse moved, the ball released a spring and the lid would fly open while a flag waved above and a bell rang for assistance. This contraption sounds pretty silly, but Collins and Karnicki had a point when you consider that at least one person was buried alive every week in America at the beginning of this century!

One such victim was a young woman who lived near Indianapolis. When she collapsed six doctors signed the death certificate after making the usual tests, but her young brother refused to believe them. He tried to prevent her body being removed for the funeral several days later, and in the struggle a bandage came loose round her jaw and it could be seen that her lips were moving.

'What do you want, what do you want?' cried the boy.

'Water,' she whispered faintly. She revived and lived to an old age.

Another American woman, the respected matron of a large orphanage, was declared dead and her body placed in a shroud before she was rescued and revived by friends. Needless to say, extra precautions were taken the next time she was presumed to be dead, but again her body was shrouded. Luckily, the undertaker happened to pierce her body with a pin, and noticed that a small drop of blood oozed from the puncture, to the joy of her friends who helped her recover. These women were fortunate – just imagine the numbers of people who were not rescued in time! It is a grisly thought.

Earlier in history, there was the case of the Grand Inquisitor of Spain. His heart was revealed while he was being embalmed, and was seen to be beating. At this moment the Cardinal regained consciousness and even tried to reach forward and grasp the embalmer's knife before he sank back and 'died' again.

This incident is echoed horrifically by a case in our own time, of a patient whose kidneys were being removed for a transplant, when it was discovered that the 'corpse' was alive. This happened in Birmingham in 1973. Just think – if we can make such mistakes with all our modern science and medical knowledge, how easy it must have been a few hundred years ago when people did not understand states of trance which look like death. Catalepsy, for example, can make the body go rigid, but it is really a form of suspended animation, and can last for several weeks.

No wonder that a doctor signed a death certificate in Moravia (now part of Czechoslovakia) when a postman was thought to have died from epilepsy. A few years later, when the bodies had to be removed from this particular graveyard, it was discovered that the postman had been buried alive – the guilt-stricken doctor was never the same man again.

Premature burial was once so commonplace in Britain that the Burial Reformer published the following verse:

> 'There was a young man at Nunhead
> Who awoke in his coffin of lead.
> "It is cosy enough,"
> He remarked in a huff,
> "But I wasn't aware I was dead."'

When the bodies of people who were buried alive were dug up, or disturbed by grave-robbers or body-snatchers, it was discovered that they had moved. Sometimes there might be blood round the mouth where the wretched person had bitten himself in a final agony, and this gave rise to the belief that they were vampires. In some cases there were signs that the shroud had been eaten in a last desperate attempt to stay alive, and although it is more likely that it was devoured by insects, wild stories can spread like wildfire and grow more fantastic in the telling.

In other words, a belief in vampirism might well have been a form of mass hysteria. This would have been especially likely in times of plague, when people would have been anxious for a scapegoat to blame. Also, there was a natural fear of disease during plague outbreaks and a wish to bury bodies as quickly as possible.

When the cholera epidemic swept across Europe at the start of the last century, it reached as far as County Sligo in the west of Ireland. A girl called Charlotte Thornley lived there with her parents. Years later, she remembered two strange incidents – first there was the soldier called Sergeant Callan, who was such a giant of a man that no coffin would hold him after he died from cholera. When an undertaker took a hammer to break his legs, in order to squeeze him in, the Sergeant sprang back to life and Charlotte saw him afterwards walking around (with a limp, presumably)!

The second case concerned a man whose wife had died after he carried her to the hospital on his back, with a red handkerchief tied round her waist to ease the pain. During this emergency, it was the practice to throw as many as fifty corpses into a trench and cover them with lime, to stop infection. Searching for his wife to give her a proper

*Vampires*

burial, the man noticed a corner of the red handkerchief, and when he lifted her body, he discovered that she was still alive. 'He carried her home,' Charlotte remembered, 'and she recovered and lived for many years.'

By this time Charlotte had grown up and married an Irish civil servant called Abraham Stoker. They had a son called Bram, who was a sickly child and bedridden for the first eight years of his life. His mother's memories of the plague may have been his bedtime stories too, giving him his first taste for horror. Years later, as Bram Stoker, he wrote the greatest vampire story of all – *Dracula* (see Chapter 4).

## The man in Stoke-on-Trent

Are vampires imaginary? Because people want to believe in something, they are sometimes prepared to believe in anything. But if vampires are nothing more than make-believe, what of official reports by the 'experts in law'?

The French philosopher Jean-Jacques Rousseau, who lived in the eighteenth century, declared: 'If ever there was in the world a warranted and proven history, it is that of vampires. Nothing is lacking: official reports, testimonials of persons of standing, of surgeons, of clergymen, of judges; the judicial evidence is all-embracing.' Dom Calmet, who did his best to keep an open mind, agreed: 'It seems impossible not to subscribe to the prevailing belief that these apparitions do actually come forth from their graves.' But, as police would confirm, eyewitnesses may be sincere but are notoriously unreliable. They are often just as mistaken as the Irish villagers who saw 'a white lady' cross a bridge at midnight – she proved to be a swan! The Croglin Grange vampire is a good story, but is it anything more? Surely Tinka's father was not dead when they started to prepare him for the funeral, but simply in a trance and in no danger of becoming a vampire?

It is all too easy to dismiss vampires when you do not believe in them, but to those who do believe, they are terrifyingly real. An extraordinary example is the man who believed he was being attacked by vampires – not in Transylvania in the eighteenth century but in Stoke-on-Trent in 1973! One night in January a young Police Constable, John Pye, was called out to investigate the death of a Pole, Demetrious Myiciura, who worked as a potter and rented a room at Number 3 The Villas – an avenue of large, old-fashioned, rather faded houses.

The room was unusual – for one thing there were no electric light bulbs. As P.C. Pye's flashlight slowly revealed the scene, he suspected he was in a sort of fortress, prepared against attack by vampires. Salt was scattered round the room and sprinkled over the bed, and bags of it lay beside the dead man's face and body. Among other precautions, a bowl containing garlic rested on the window-ledge.

At first the pathologist's report suggested that the man had died from bolting his food, as a pickled onion was found sticking in his throat, However, P.C. Pye had shown the initiative of going to the Public Library and taking out a book called *Natural History of the Vampire* by Anthony Masters, which confirmed his suspicion that salt and garlic are traditional ways of scaring off vampires. The coroner ordered a closer examination and P.C. Pye was proved right – the pickled onion was really a clove of garlic which the man placed in his mouth at night as a final safeguard before going to sleep. He had choked on it and died.

Vampires *did* exist to this man and, in a strange sort of way, they *did* get him in the end. But are there such things? Who knows?

# 3
# WERE-WOLVES

'*Does your head become like that of a wolf?*'
'*I do not know how my head was at the time;
I used my teeth.*'

(Cross-examination of a 'werewolf'
in 1598)

### The legend of the werewolf

A werewolf is a man or woman who can change into a wolf. The translation from the early Anglo-Saxon is simple: *wer* means man, *wulf* is wolf. There are three types of werewolf – the true werewolf, the *lycanthrope* (someone who thinks he is a wolf and behaves like one) and a strange and gruesome third version – a human being who looks ordinary on the outside but whose skin is inside-out! In olden days, hundreds of innocent people were torn apart to see if there they were furry inside:

> *'Two nights since*
> *One met the duke 'bout midnight in a lane*
> *Behind Saint Mark's Church, with the leg of a man*
> *Upon his shoulder; and he howled fearfully,*
> *Said he was a wolf, only the difference*
> *Was, a wolf's skin was hairy on the outside*
> *His, on the inside!*
>
> (from *The Duchess of Malfi*, 1623,
> by John Webster)

The werewolf and the vampire have much in common. It was generally believed that a werewolf became a vampire after death, unless special precautions were taken.

How did people become werewolves? All too easily! If you ate part of a sheep that had been killed by a wolf, or drank water from a wolf's footprints, it was said that you were likely to become a werewolf. Mind you, it is dangerous to eat the flesh of *any* animal killed by a wolf or fox, for you could become infected by rabies. If this had happened long ago, and the person foamed at the mouth, he might well have been considered a wolf. As for drinking

## Werewolves

from a wolf's footprints, you'd have to be odd to do that in the first place!

How did you recognise a werewolf? If you met someone who had pointed ears, hair on the palms of his hands, curved fingernails or eyebrows that met in the middle, you would have to take care! The eyes of a werewolf always stayed human.

Basically, belief in werewolves can be explained by the ignorant fear of anyone different. Even so, many people wanted to become werewolves, and were prepared to suffer elaborate rituals to do so. The right moment for the transformation was midnight, by the light of the full moon. It was supposed to help if you smeared yourself with the fat of a newly-killed cat mixed with aniseed, and wore a belt of wolf's skin. In Russia, the would-be wolf knelt inside a circle while the magic potions simmered. He chanted a tribute to the wolf spirit:

> *Make me a werewolf strong and bold,*
> *The terror alike of young and old.*
> *Grant me a figure tall and spare;*
> *The speed of the elk, the claws of the bear;*
> *The poison of snakes, the wit of the fox;*
> *The stealth of the wolf, the strength of the ox;*
> *The jaws of the tiger, the teeth of the shark;*
> *The eyes of a cat that sees in the dark.*

The chant ends with the horrific shout:

> *Make me a werewolf! make me a man-eater!*
> *Make me a werewolf! make me a woman-eater!*
> *Make me a werewolf! make me a child-eater!*
> *I pine for blood! human blood!*

> *Give it to me! Give it to me tonight!*
> *Great Wolf Spirit! give it to me, and*
> *Heart, body, and soul, I am yours.*

Don't bother to try this – it won't work! It was supposed to conjure up a figure which glowed in the darkness until it assumed the form of 'a tall thin monstrosity, half human and half animal, grey and nude, with very long legs and arms, and the feet and claws of a wolf.' From then on, the man or woman became a werewolf at sunset and returned to human shape at dawn by rolling in the dew. This continued until death or until the werewolf was shot by a silver bullet. Then the body had to be buried, never burnt.

All this was primitive superstition. Reports of werewolves were most common in wild regions where the wolf was feared as a dangerous animal. As cities spread into the countryside, werewolves started to disappear. Werewolves fitted neatly into ancient folklore – a good tale for the fireside on long winter nights when there was little else to talk about, apart from the wild animals of the forest and the wilder characters in the villages. Just as London cockneys warned their children not to wander in the East End streets after dark, after the murders of 1888 ('or Jack the Ripper will get you'), it was natural for peasants to threaten their children: 'Don't go out in the woods tonight or a werewolf will gobble you up.' True enough – a real wolf might!

So, are there such things as werewolves? Surprisingly, a number of people have taken the legend seriously. In *Book of were wolves, Being an account of a terrible Superstition* (1865), Sabine Baring-Gould said that the legend was so persistent 'everywhere and in all ages, it must rest upon

## Werewolves

foundation of fact.' He even claimed: 'Half the world believes, or believed in were-wolves.'

Like vampirism, reports of werewolves have been reported since the beginning of time. Herodotus, who lived in the 5th century B.C. and was known as 'the father of history', wrote: 'Each Neurian changes himself once a year into the form of a wolf and he continues in that form for several days, after which he resumes his former shape.' Ovid, the Latin poet (43 B.C. to A.D. 18), wrote of a king who was transformed by the gods:

> 'In vain he attempted to speak; from that very instant his jaws were/Bespluttered with foam, and he thirsted for blood, as he raged/Amongst flocks and panted for slaughter/His vesture was changed into hair, his limbs became crooked;/A wolf, he retains yet large trace of his ancient expression/Hoary he is as afore, his countenance rabid,/His eyes glitter savagely still, the picture of fury.

The reference to his 'rabid' appearance is intriguing, suggesting that the man was suffering from a form of rabies.

One of the classic werewolf stories was told by Petronius, a Roman in the first century, whose account has a universal theme. A servant accompanied a soldier one night on a journey out of town. He was aghast to see the soldier strip off his clothes by the roadside and change instantly into a wolf. With a howl, the creature leapt into the woods and the servant picked up the clothes, only to find they had turned into stone. Continuing to his destination, the servant was told that if he had arrived a moment earlier he could have helped in fighting off a wolf which had broken into the farm and killed cattle until driven away by a man with a sword, which he had thrust into the animal. Hurrying back home, the servant came to the place where the soldier's clothes had been left – now there was only a pool of blood. At home he found the soldier, wounded by a sword-thrust, with a surgeon dressing his neck.

This sort of story has been echoed through the ages. In 1558, a hunter in the French forests of Auvergne met a nobleman who was one of his neighbours and who asked him to bring some game if he was lucky. Later, the hunter was attacked by a savage wolf but was able to drive it away after slashing one of its paws. Returning home, he remembered his friend and called at his château to tell him of the adventure. At the end of his story he took out the wolf's paw, which he had put in his pouch as a trophy, but to his amazement it was no longer a paw but a delicate feminine hand. The nobleman started back, recognising the gold ring on one of the fingers. He raced upstairs to find his wife bandaging the bleeding stump of her wrist. She confessed and was burnt at the stake at Rouen.

Just as Transylvania was the home of the vampire, central France was famous for *loups garoux*, as the werewolves were known. As many as 30,000 cases were listed between 1520 and 1630. Many of these came to trial. On 13th September, 1573, the Parlement at Dole authorised a werewolf hunt after several local children disappeared:

'And since he has attacked and done injury to some horsemen, who kept him off only with great difficulty and danger to their persons, the said court has permitted those who are dwelling in the said places to assemble with pikes, halberds, and sticks to chase and pursue the said werewolf in every place where they may find or seize him; to tie and to kill, without incurring any penalties.'

It seems extraordinary that no one suspected a real wolf!

Two months later, the werewolf hunters heard the screams of a child and the baying of a wolf. Hurrying to the spot, they found a small girl and thought they recognised a man called Gilles Garnier in the 'wolf' that raced away. When a ten-year-old boy disappeared six days later, they raided the hut of the lonely Garnier, who was known as 'the hermit of St Bonnot', and arrested him and his wife.

Garnier confessed at once. He admitted killing a boy the previous August, and a ten-year-old girl in an orchard. He said he appeared in the form of a wolf and attacked her with his teeth and claws. He enjoyed eating her so much that he brought some of the flesh back for his wife's supper. On this evidence, Garnier was burnt alive on 18th January, 1574.

### The case of Jean Grenier

Accused 'werewolves' were surprisingly keen to confess. Obviously, torture helped them on, but sometimes it seemed as if they wanted to. A fourteen-year-old shepherd called Jean Grenier is an interesting example. His crimes took place near Bordeaux, thirty years after those of Garnier and, for what his confession is worth, he admitted to having eaten more than fifty children. He confessed with such pleasure that the crowded courtroom burst into laughter when he described chasing an old woman only to find her flesh 'as tough as leather'. When he lifted a child from its cot, he complained that 'it shrieked so loud it almost deafened me' as he prepared for his first bite. Hardly the stuff to take seriously, but three girls testified against him, and his detailed confession was believed though the judge found the evidence so appalling that he sent Grenier to a higher court.

Grenier was sentenced to be burnt, but by now the case had caused such a stir – with further confessions – that it was sent to an even higher court, where the judge showed surprising common sense. First he recorded Grenier's story: 'When I was ten or eleven years old, my neighbour introduced me in the depths of the forest, to the *Maître de la Forêt* [master of the forest] who gave me a wolf skin. From that time I have run about the country as a wolf.' The judge called in two doctors, who decided that Grenier was suffering from 'a malady called lycanthropy which deceives men's eyes into imagining such things'. The judge gave a wise summing-up, which could explain all those confessions and cases of werewolves:

> 'The court takes into account the young age and the imbecility of this boy, who is so stupid and idiotic that children of seven and eight years old normally show more intelligence, who has been ill fed in every respect and who is so dwarfed that he is not as tall as a ten year old ... Here is a young lad abandoned and driven out by his father, who has a cruel stepmother instead of a real mother, who wanders over the fields, without a counsellor and without anyone to take an interest in him, begging his bread, who has never had any religious training, whose real nature was corrupted by evil promptings, need, and despair, and whom the devil made his prey.'

The boy was spared. He was sent to a monastery which the judge visited seven years later. He found that Grenier was unable to understand the simplest things, but still insisted that he was a werewolf.

### The beggar werewolf
Another merciful verdict, for those days, was granted to a beggar called Roulet at Angers in 1598. He was found half-naked in some bushes, with long hair, nails like claws, and hands clotted with blood, after a boy's body had been discovered in the woods and a wolf seen racing away.

'I was a wolf,' Roulet confessed to the court.

'Do your hands and feet become paws?'

'Yes, they do.'

'Does your head become like that of a wolf?'

'I do not know how my head was at the time; I used my teeth.'

He was sentenced to a madhouse, but only for two years.

### The werewolves of St Claude
This case was recorded in 1588, and concerned a family of 'werewolves' – two sisters, their brother and his son. The latter testified that he had covered himself with a magic salve which had turned him into a wolf and had then gone hunting with his aunts (a nice family touch!) and killed two goats.

The judge visited this family in jail and saw them walk about the room on all fours as if they were in a field, '... but they said it was impossible for them to turn themselves into wolves, since they had no more ointment, and they had lost the power of doing so by being imprisoned.' He noticed that Pierre Gandillon, the boy's father, was so scratched about the face that he hardly resembled a man, 'and struck with horror those who looked at him'. This last point reveals a great deal. If Pierre had been disfigured since birth, it is understandable that he preferred the company of animals and tried to avoid his fellow men. This time the verdict was unmerciful – the family was burned to death.

## The German werewolf

The most famous German werewolf, Peter Stubb, was tried in Cologne in 1589. He claimed he had a magic belt which transformed him into 'a greedy, devouring wolf, strong and mighty, with eyes great and large, which in the night sparkled like brands of fire, a mouth great and wide, with most sharp and cruel teeth, a huge body and mighty paws.' Lawyers searched the valley where he said he had left his belt, but nothing was found. In spite of this they believed his confession and decided that the belt had been taken by the devil. Their revenge was terrible. Stubb was condemned to have 'his body laid on a wheel, and with red hot burning pincers in ten several places to have the flesh pulled from his bones; after that, his legs and arms to be broken with a wooden axe or hatchet; afterwards to have his head struck off from his body; then to have his carcase burned to ashes.' Even vampires were treated better than that!

## The werewolf and the sea captain

A French sea captain was employed in fighting the Huguenots, the Protestants who were persecuted by the Catholics in the seventeenth century, and many of whom fled to England. After a raid his ship filled with water and started to sink in the Rhône estuary. The captain would have drowned, but someone came to his rescue and brought him to shore. Reaching out his hand gratefully, he was horrified to find himself grasping a hairy paw. He fell on his knees, thinking he had been saved by the Devil as a reward for his attacks on the Huguenots.

While the captain asked the forgiveness of God, the wolf waited grimly. He then led him to a house, where he gave him food before locking him in a barred room. The captain saw the dead body of a woman in the corner, and thought this would be his fate as well. But in the morning the werewolf returned in the shape of a Huguenot clergyman, and explained that the woman was his wife, murdered by the captain's crew when they had raided the village the day before. He continued:

'Yes, I am a werewolf. I was bewitched some years ago by the woman Grenier [that name again] who lives in the forest. I saw you drowning. I saved you . . . you who had been instrumental in murdering my wife and ruining my home. Why? I do not know. Had I preferred a less pleasant death for you than drowning, I could have taken you ashore and killed you. Yet I did not, because it is not my nature to destroy anything!'

The captain was so impressed that he became a champion of the Huguenot cause until the day of his death.

### Saved by a werewolf!
Nice and romantic and unlikely, yet this story might have a basis of truth. Wolves have always been known as wild killers, but this is untrue. It has been discovered recently that wolves only attack man when they are attacked themselves, and they have often been known to save a man's life. One old story concerns an abbot who drank too much cider at a country fair and was overcome by the sun on his journey back. Half-asleep, he fell off his horse, hitting his

head on a stone. He bled so profusely that the scent attracted a pack of wild cats from the forest. A werewolf bounded to his rescue and escorted the drowsy abbot to the monastery. At dawn it assumed human shape again and turned out to be a churchman who lectured the abbot severely for his conduct the day before and stripped him of all his privileges. A protective werewolf, admittedly, but a bossy one!

The helpful werewolf is also the theme of *Dracula's Guest*, which Bram Stoker wrote as the opening chapter of his novel. He cut it from the finished novel, but his wife published it after his death.

Travelling on his way to Castle Dracula, Jonathan Harker collapses at midnight on Walpurgis Nacht (the night when all evil things have sway) in the extreme cold of a graveyard:

> 'A vast stillness enveloped me, as though all the world were asleep or dead, only broken by the low panting as of some animal close to me. I felt a warm rasping at my throat, then came a consciousness of the awful truth, which chilled me to the heart and sent the blood surging up through my brain. Some great animal was lying on me and now licking my throat. I feared to stir, for some instinct of prudence bade me lie still; but the brute seemed to realise that there was now some change in me for it raised its head. Through my eyelashes I saw above me the two great flaming eyes of a gigantic wolf. Its sharp white teeth gleamed in the gaping red mouth, and I could feel its hot breath fierce and acrid upon me.'

A search party has been looking for Harker, and some cavalrymen now ride into the graveyard and disturb the wolf, who bounds away over the snow. Presumably this was Count Dracula himself, in the shape of a werewolf, and he has saved Harker's life by lying on his body and keeping him warm.

The *metamorphosis* – the change of a man into animal – was an early legend, a gift of the gods. The Scandinavian God Odin became an eagle, Jupiter, the Roman god, a bull and Actaeon a stag. The idea of a wer-wulf, man into wolf, was common all over the world, though the shape varied according to the climate – were-tigers in India, were-leopards in Africa and were-bears in Russia. These are always fierce animals – you never hear of a were-dormouse!

## What are they really?

Are there logical explanations for werewolves? Yes, of course. One of the most obvious is that werewolves were really children lost in the forest, or left there deliberately, and found by packs of wolves who brought them up with their own cubs, teaching them all the hunting skills of the wild animals (see Chapter 6). Another explanation is even simpler – the *Berserkirs*, gangs of Nordic warriors, profited from the wild reputation of the bear by dressing in his skin ('bear-sark' means bear-skin). They prayed to the spirits of the bear and the wolf in the hope of gaining the animal's strength, and then worked themselves into a state of frenzy as they raided remote villages, howling like wolves. 'Going berserk', a phrase they have given to the language, is defined by the dictionary as a 'murderous frenzy'. It is understandable that ignorant villagers, glimpsing them as they howled by in the darkness of night dressed in animal skins, might wonder what they were, and talk of them afterwards as half-man, half-animal.

1 Unharmed by a spear thrown at him, a werewolf snatches up a young woman and carries her off in his jaws.

2 (*above*) and 3 (*below*) Mary Shelley was only nineteen when she wrote *Frankenstein*. Looming over her portrait is Frankenstein's monster as portrayed by Boris Karloff in the 1931 film. Note the plug in his neck and the 'straight black lips'.

Unfriendly reactions to two more 'monsters' – 4 (*above*) townspeople shrink back in horror as Quasimodo shuffles by – a still from the 1931 film of *The Hunchback of Notre Dame*, with Charles Laughton in the leading role; 5 (*below*) King Kong reaches up and deposits the terrified girl in a tree – from the 1933 film.

6 (*above*) Edgar Allan Poe's private life was a nightmare which inspired him to write his tales of horror.

7 (*below*) The American Ambrose Bierce hated being compared to Poe – his stories have no trace of the humanity shown by Poe.

8 A dramatic illustration of the climax of Poe's story *William Wilson*, as the 'real' Wilson plunges his sword into his 'double'.

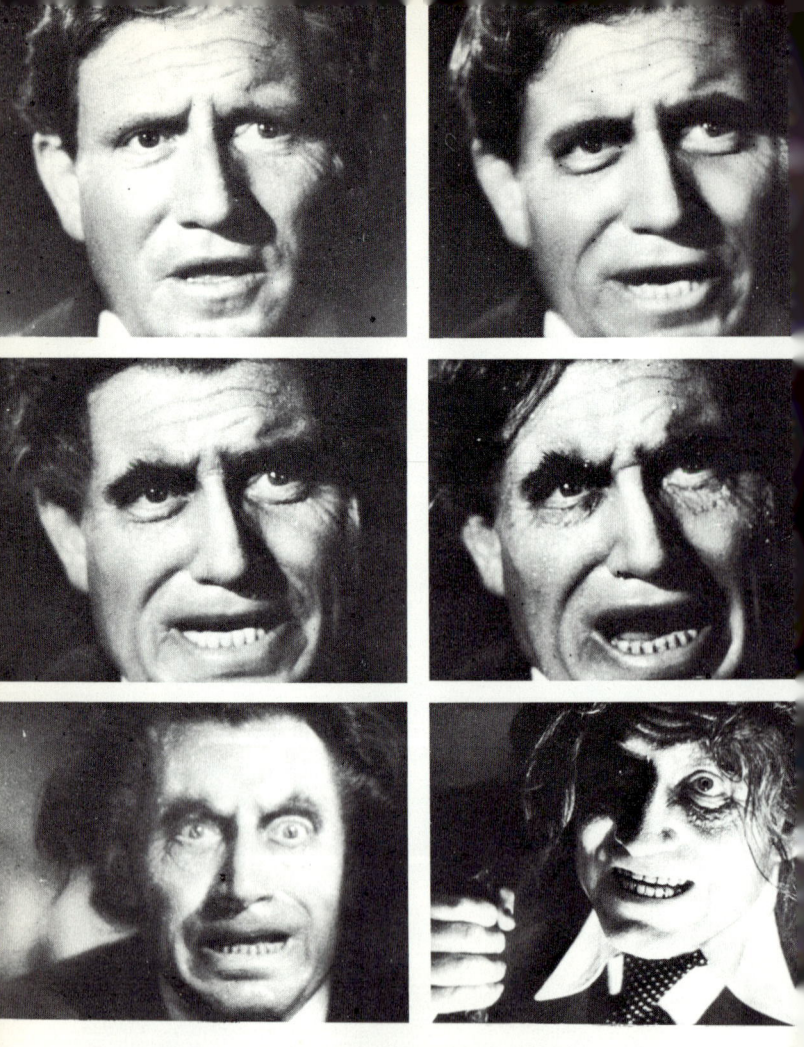

9 'There is something wrong with his appearance; something displeasing, something downright detestable. I never saw a man I so disliked, and yet I scarce know why...' (*The Strange Case of Dr Jekyll and Mr Hyde*). These shots from the 1941 film show Jekyll's transformation into Hyde. The actor is Spencer Tracy.

10 Stevenson probably drew on personal experience when he wrote his masterpiece of horror, *The Strange Case of Dr Jekyll and Mr Hyde*, for throughout his life he was tormented by his conscience.

11 'The Man of a Thousand Faces' in one of his most famous roles – Lon Chaney in the 1925 film of *The Phantom of the Opera*.

# 4 HORROR STORIES

'If it scares you to read that one imaginary person killed another, why not take up knitting?'

(Ambrose Bierce,
American writer and
master of the macabre)

Some horror stories seem so familiar, like *Frankenstein*, that people think they have read the book even when they haven't. For instance, how many of you think that 'Frankenstein' is the name of the monster, when it is really his creator, Baron Frankenstein? Did you know that Count Dracula had a white moustache, or that Mr Hyde had rooms in London's Soho?

It would be silly to list the best horror stories in any order, as if it were an Ugly Contest, but it is fair to claim that the three most celebrated horror books in literature are *Dracula* by Bram Stoker, born in Dublin; *The Strange Case of Dr Jekyll and Mr Hyde* by Robert Louis Stevenson, born in Edinburgh; and *Frankenstein* by Mary Shelley, the wife of the poet.

Count Dracula revives life, Baron Frankenstein creates it, and Dr Jekyll shows the conflict inside us between good and evil. These books deal with universal themes of life and death, which explains their lasting popularity. Their names are better known today than when they were written.

Read the great originals, and discover how different they are from what you imagine.

**Classic horror stories**
*Ten novels:*

Frankenstein   *Mary Shelley*
Dracula   *Bram Stoker*
The Werewolf of Paris   *Guy Endore*
The Witch of Prague   *F. Marion Crawford*
The Prisoner in the Opal   *A. E. W. Mason*
Uncle Silas   *Sheridan Le Fanu*
The Phantom of the Opera   *Gaston Leroux*

## Horror Stories

The Strange Case of Dr Jekyll and Mr Hyde *Robert Louis Stevenson*
The Picture of Dorian Gray   *Oscar Wilde*
The Turn of the Screw   *Henry James*


*Ten short stories:*

The Tell-tale Heart   *Edgar Allan Poe*
Green Tea   *Sheridan Le Fanu*
The Horla   *Guy de Maupassant*
The Damned Thing   *Ambrose Bierce*
The Monkey's Paw   *W. W. Jacobs*
The Squaw   *Bram Stoker*
'Oh, Whistle, and I'll Come to You My Lad'   *M. R. James*
The Speckled Band   *Sir Arthur Conan Doyle*
Mrs Amworth   *E. F. Benson*
William and Mary   *Raoul Dahl*


*Ten more to look out for:*

Man Sized in Marble   *E. Nesbitt*
The Man Upstairs   *Ray Bradbury*
The Man Who Didn't Ask Why   *C. S. Forester*
At the End of the Passage   *Rudyard Kipling*
The Prowler in the City at the Edge of the World   *Harlan Ellison*
Yours Truly Jack the Ripper   *Robert Bloch*
The Hound   *H. P. Lovecraft*
The Body Snatchers   *Robert Louis Stevenson*
The Haunted and the Haunters   *Bulwer Lytton*
The Dancing Partner   *Jerome K. Jerome*

## Frankenstein

*Frankenstein* is one of the strangest books ever written, and the fact that Mary Shelley was only nineteen when she wrote it makes it all the stranger.

The story takes the form of letters written by a man called Robert Walton to his sister Margaret. He writes the first one from St Petersburg in Russia, dated 11th December, 17— (the exact year is not given). In his second letter he tells her that he has hired a ship at Archangel and is busy collecting a crew to sail her to the North Pole. He is an unlikely sea captain, an odd, lonely character, very much an outsider.

The following summer Walton finds a friend in Viktor Frankenstein. They meet in the Arctic wastes of the North Pole. The ship has been closed in by ice on every side, when the crew notices a sledge, drawn by dogs and guided by a gigantic figure, passing northwards. That night the ice breaks up and a fragment drifts towards the ship the following morning. On it is a sledge, one dog, and a man who is nearly frozen to death. When he has recovered, Captain Walton asks why he has come so far on the ice in so strange a vehicle.

'To seek one who fled from me,' replies the stranger.

'And did the man whom you pursued travel in the same fashion?'

'Yes.'

'Then I fancy we have seen him,' says Walton. This news excites the stranger, but he seems to be suffering terribly. He asks the Captain to listen to his story.

Viktor Frankenstein (for that is the name of the stranger) was born in Naples but brought up in Geneva. His parents are devoted to him, and their foster child, Elizabeth, becomes his adored companion. He is a brilliant child. At the age of fourteen he becomes obsessed by the 'secrets of heaven and earth' and the search for an 'elixir of life', which will prolong it indefinitely.

When he is seventeen, Frankenstein goes to the University of Ingelstadt, where he is able to continue his studies. At night he learns about anatomy in 'charnel houses' or mortuaries and graveyards. At last he is able to announce, 'I succeeded in discovering the cause of generation and life; nay, more, I became myself capable of bestowing animation upon lifeless matter.' He starts to build a frame that will hold his manufactured man, who is to be eight feet (nearly 2.5 metres) tall and proportionately large, constructed from bones he collects from the mortuary, the slaughter-house and the dissecting-room of a hospital.

*'It was on a dreary night of November that I beheld the accomplishment of my toils.'* Originally, this was the opening line of the novel – Frankenstein's first sight of the monster. He realises his experiment is a catastrophe.

> 'Great God! His yellow skin scarcely covered the work of muscles and arteries beneath; his hair was of a lustrous black, and flowing; his teeth of a pearly whiteness; but these luxuriances only formed a more horrid contrast with his watery eyes, that seemed almost of the same colour as the dun white sockets in which they were set, his shrivelled complexion and straight black lips.'

With his 'instruments of life' around him, he sees the creature open its eyes: '... it breathed hard, and a convulsive motion agitated its limbs.'

After working hard for two years, Frankenstein's hopes are shattered. He rushes to the safety of his bedroom, where he falls asleep and dreams that he sees the corpse of Elizabeth, his foster-sister. He wakes up to find the monster watching him. 'He held up the curtain of the bed; and his eyes, if eyes they may be called, were fixed on me. His jaws opened, and he muttered some inarticulate sounds, while a grin wrinkled his cheeks.'

Frankenstein escapes from the house. While he is walking through the streets, he meets his boyhood friend, Henry Clerval, and they return to Frankenstein's lodgings. At first he is wildly relieved to find that the monster has gone, then he imagines it is attacking him, and falls down in a fit.

He is ill with fever the whole winter. When he recovers, he receives sad news from his father in Switzerland – his little brother William has been found murdered. A miniature of their mother, which the boy used to wear, is found in the clothes of a servant girl who is arrested as the main suspect.

Frankenstein hurries back home, and as he is walking through the forest on the last part of his journey, a flash of lightning reveals the monster. He becomes convinced that the monster murdered William. Together with Elizabeth, he protests the innocence of the servant girl, Justine, but she is found guilty and hanged. He is sick with guilt: '... torn by remorse, horror and despair, I beheld those I loved spend vain sorrow upon the graves of William and Justine, the first hapless victims to my unhallowed arts.'

Frankenstein meets the monster again in the mountains of Chamonix. Trembling with rage and horror, he rejects him cruelly:

'Devil ... Begone, vile insect! Or rather, stay, that I may trample you to dust!'

The monster makes a poignant plea for friendship: 'Be

calm! I entreat you to hear me.... Have I not suffered enough, that you seek to increase my misery?' He reminds him that he is stronger than his creator, but refuses to hurt him. 'Oh, Frankenstein,' he implores him pathetically, 'be not equitable to every other, and trample upon me alone, to whom thy justice, and even thy clemency and affection is most due. Remember, that I am thy creature; I ought to be thy Adam; but I am rather the fallen angel, whom thou drivest from joy for no misdeed. Everywhere I see bliss, from which I alone am irrevocably excluded. I was benevolent and good; misery made me a fiend. Make me happy, and I shall again be virtuous.' But his plea for kindness goes unheard. He describes his fate – miserably alone, shunned by man and condemned to wander in the desert mountains and dreary glaciers. He threatens that if he does not receive Frankenstein's friendship, he will make mankind share his wretchedness: '... not only you and your family, but thousands of others, shall be swallowed up in the whirlwind of its rage.'

Does Frankenstein agree to the monster's demands? If you want to find out what happens (and plenty does!) you will have to read Mary Shelley's novel.

Mary Shelley was known as Mary Wollstonecraft Godwin at the time she wrote this novel. Her father, William Godwin, was a famous political philosopher. Her mother, Mary Wollstonecraft, was one of the earliest champions of rights for women.

Mary was born on 30th August, 1797. Many of her early years were spent in Scotland, near Dundee. She remembered the place later as 'blank and dreary', but at the time she had the freedom to move in a fantasy world, talking to 'the creatures of my fancy'.

Her friendship with the Romantic poet, Percy Bysshe Shelley, began when she was only fifteen. He was five years older and married. When she was seventeen, she eloped with Shelley and they travelled through France to Switzerland, spending the summer of 1816 on the shores of Lake Geneva. Their neighbour was Shelley's close friend, the poet Lord Byron. While Byron spent the day at work writing, they boated on the lake or walked around it until the weather grew so bad that it kept them indoors. Luckily some books of ghost stories kept them amused, and one day Byron suggested that they should each write their own. The two poets soon gave up, and as for Mary, nothing came into her head, though she tried to think of a story 'which would speak to the mysterious fears of our nature, and awaken thrilling horror – one to make the reader dread to look round, to curdle the blood, and quicken the beatings of the heart'. Decidedly bloodthirsty for a girl of eighteen!

'Have you thought of a story?' they asked her when she came down each morning, and she had to say 'no'.

While the two great poets talked, she listened. One of their conversations was about the experiments concerning the origin of Man carried out by a scientist related to Charles Darwin. Darwin claimed that Man was not created, as the Bible suggests, but descended from the same family as the apes. The poets wondered if the 'principle of life' would ever be discovered.

One of these experiments made use of a piece of Italian 'pasta', like spaghetti, called *vermicelli* (which means 'little worm'). This was placed in a glass case until 'by some extraordinary means it began to move with voluntary motion'. This led Mary to her tremendous idea: '... perhaps a corpse would be re-animated ... perhaps the component parts of a creature might be manufactured, brought together, and endued with vital warmth'. That night she was unable to sleep. In a sort of waking dream, she saw 'with shut eyes, but acute mental vision ... the hideous phantasm of a man stretched out, and then, on the working of some powerful engine, show signs of life, and stir with an uneasy, half vital motion. His success would terrify the artist; he would rush away from his odious handiwork, horror stricken. He would hope that, left to itself, the slight spark of life which he had communicated would fade ... He sleeps; but he is awakened; he opens his eyes; behold the horrid thing stands at his bedside, opening his curtains and looking on him with yellow, watery, but speculative eyes.'

Mary opened her own eyes with terror, and remembered her ghost story. When she came downstairs the next morning, she was able to tell the others she had thought of her story: 'I began that day with the words, *It was on a dreary night of November*, making only a transcript of the grim terrors of my waking dream.'

The game round the blazing wood fire, when each of them had agreed to write about the supernatural, had become serious. Shelley urged her to write a long novel rather than a short story, and she was the first to admit that, but for him, 'it would never have taken the form in which it was presented to the world.'

She completed *Frankenstein* the following May and it was published in March 1818. At the end of 1816, Shelley's wife died (by committing suicide), and he married Mary on 30th December. But tragedy pursued them, with the deaths of their baby daughter and son. In November 1819 another son was born, and survived, but less than three years later Shelley was drowned at sea off the coast of Italy. His body was burnt in a funeral pyre on the beach near Lerici and his ashes buried in Rome. Mary Shelley wrote other books, but none caused the sensation of *Frankenstein*. She died in 1851 and is buried at Bournemouth. Like Bram Stoker, the author of *Dracula*, she wrote a story that has become a household name, but she herself is hardly remembered.

## The Hunchback of Notre Dame

This story was written in 1831 by the great French novelist Victor Hugo under the original title of *Notre-Dame de Paris*. On one level it is a romantic historical novel, set in the great cathedral of Paris in 1482, but it is also the universal story of beauty and the beast.

Though you are urged to read the original novel, be warned that the hunchback, Quasimodo, does not appear until Chapter Three of Book Four. He is discovered by Claude Frollo, the youngest chaplain of Notre Dame, who returns from saying Mass on Quasimodo Sunday and is shocked to see a group of old women tormenting a foundling child:

> 'The poor little imp had a great wart covering its left eye – the head compressed between the shoulders – the spine crooked – the breastbone prominent – and the legs bowed. Yet it seemed to be full of life ... Claude's compassion was increased by this ugliness; and he vowed in his heart to bring up this child ...'

So Quasimodo is saved, but fate continues to pursue him. At the age of fourteen the sound of the great cathedral bells breaks his eardrums and he becomes deaf. From then on the outside world is closed to him, and the cathedral becomes a place to hide in. Ironically, the only thing he can hear is the ringing of the bells:

> 'This was the only speech that he could hear, the only sound that broke for him the universal silence. He expanded in it, like a bird in the sunshine. All at once the frenzy of the bell would seize him; his look became wild – he lay in wait for the great bell as a spider for a fly, and then flung himself headlong upon it. Now, suspended over the abyss, borne to and fro by the formidable swinging of the bell, he seized the brazen monster by the ears – gripped it with his knees – spurred it with his heels – and redoubled, with the shock and weight of his body, the fury of the peal. Meanwhile, the tower trembled; he shouted and gnashed his teeth – his red hair bristled – his breast heaved and puffed like the bellows of a forge – his eye flashed fire – the monstrous bell neighed panting beneath him. Then it was no longer the great bell of Notre-Dame, nor Quasimodo – it was a dream – a whirl – a tempest – dizziness astride upon clamour – a strange centaur, half-man, half-bell – a spirit clinging to a winged monster ...'

Unable to hear, hardly able to speak, Quasimodo is persecuted by people who cannot understand him and are frightened by his appearance. At one point he is flogged and placed in the pillory, pelted with stones by the mob until he is only half alive. He calls in vain for water until the beautiful gypsy girl, Esmeralda, makes her way through the crowd and lifts a gourd of water to his parched, deformed lips:

'Then in that eye, hitherto so dry and burning, a big tear was seen to start, which fell slowly down that misshapen face so long convulsed by despair. It was possibly the first that the unfortunate creature had ever shed.'

Later it is Quasimodo's turn to rescue Esmeralda from the executioner and hide her in his cell high up in the cathedral. Victor Hugo's story builds up to a tremendous climax – read it for yourself.

## Seeing double

Have you ever seen your double? Unless you hate yourself, this could be quite a pleasant experience, but it is an idea which has been used by some of the greatest masters of horror.

The ancient Egyptians used the word *Ka* to describe a person's exact duplicate. In Scotland, the *wraith* is an apparition or ghost which looks exactly like you and comes to claim you the moment before death. The Germans refer to a *doppelganger*, which means double-goer; and another expression is *alter ego*, described by the Oxford Dictionary as 'one's other self, intimate friend'.

Joseph Conrad's *The Secret Sharer*, one of the finest short stories ever written, concerns such an *alter ego*. A young inexperienced sea captain is anchored in the Gulf of Siam. Looking over the side of his ship, he notices what appears to be a headless corpse floating in the water.

In fact it is nothing of the sort, but the mate of a ship called the *Sephora*, anchored in the distance. He is wanted for murder but the captain befriends him and allows him on board – an incident which recalls the meeting of Robert Walton and Viktor Frankenstein.

Hiding him from his own crew and the *Sephora's* captain who comes looking for him, he thinks of the man as his 'double' – both of them strangers on the ship. There are several narrow escapes when the steward enters the cabin unexpectedly, but the captain manages to keep the wanted man concealed. At one moment he wonders if the man is invisible to everyone else, and remarks: 'It was like being haunted.' At the same time, he admires the stranger, who has justified the killing he has committed and intends to jump overboard and start a new life on the mainland.

When they set sail, the captain steers his ship dangerously close to the land to let his 'double' escape. The crew panic, and as the captain begins to fear they are running aground in the darkness, he notices a white object on the water – 'my own floppy hat. It must have fallen off his head.'

With the floating whiteness of the hat as a warning marker, the young captain is able to steer his ship to safety. In saving the stranger he has saved himself. He has shed all his inexperience and come of age. He looks back and catches a glimpse of his white hat – 'where the secret sharer of my cabin and of my thoughts, as though he were my second self, had lowered himself into the water to take his punishment: a free man, a proud swimmer striking out for a new destiny.'

It is a haunting story. Not horrific certainly, but a rare example of a 'second self' who comes to the rescue – a 'good angel'. Most doubles are horrible! One such example is the story which Hall Caine (one of the most successful novelists of the last century, though now almost forgotten) told Bram Stoker, the author of *Dracula*, one evening after dinner. This is more or less how he told the tale of *The Face in the Mirror*:

'I stayed the night in the proverbial haunted house, and a very cheerful house it was too, I might add. Not a rustle of a ghost. At bedtime, my host led me to a room where, so he said, another visitor had cut his throat twenty years earlier. It was a comfortable room and I slept perfectly. I rose feeling rested and started to shave with the bowl of warm water the maid had brought me. I looked into the glass above the washstand. There was the reflection – but it was not mine. I stared into the eyes of another man – it was the *wrong* face. And, at the bottom of the glass, I noticed a hand – his hand – moving slowly upwards with an open razor, towards my throat.

I am ashamed to say I screamed and ran from the room. I returned later but there was nothing, only my *own* reflection.'

'Did you recognise the man?' asked Stoker.

'No. He was a stranger. I have often wondered since what might have happened if I had stayed to watch the moving hand. I believe, also, that should I ever meet this man face to face, it will signify my death.'

Some writers, such as Robert Louis Stevenson, Edgar Allan Poe and Sheridan Le Fanu believed that the double was your *guilty conscience*. Poe and Stevenson knew what they were talking about. Both led double lives. This turmoil was reflected in their finest horror stories – *The Tell-Tale Heart* (Poe) and *The Strange Story of Dr Jekyll and Mr Hyde* (Robert Louis Stevenson).

### Edgar Allan Poe's 'tales'

Some of Poe's longer stories are very well known because they have been filmed – for example *The Fall of the House of Usher*. His work *The Murders in the Rue Morgue* has the distinction of being recognised as the first detective story. However it is fair to claim that his greatest prose is contained in the amazing short stories that reveal his guilty conscience.

*William Wilson* is a classic example of 'seeing double'. The story is told by William Wilson. There is another boy at his English school who has the same name, and the two look so alike that they are considered brothers. They even share the same birth date. The narrator's feelings towards this other Wilson are mixed – '. . . not yet hatred, some esteem, more respect, much fear, with a world of uneasy curiosity.' The only marked difference between them is that the other Wilson speaks in a very low whisper. He copies the narrator's clothes and way of walking, so irritating the latter that he tries to shake him off.

The narrator goes to Eton, but he cannot escape the other Wilson. After a wild night, with a secret party in his rooms, he is told that a stranger has called for him. Reeling towards the gates, he is clutched by a familiar figure and a voice whispers – 'William Wilson!' He adds: 'I grew perfectly sober in an instant.'

This righteous *alter ego* even pursues him to Oxford University. One night he wins a considerable amount of money cheating at cards, when the door bursts open and the other Wilson appears. With his fearful whisper, he urges the other player to examine the cuff of the narrator's left sleeve, where they find some extra cards.

He is ruined. He flees the country, but, 'My evil destiny pursued me' – to Paris – to Rome – always interrupting and wrecking his schemes. At last, coming face to face at a masked ball in Rome, he forces the other Wilson against a wall and plunges his sword, 'with brute ferocity, repeatedly through and through his bosom.'

Now he learns, as the reader has suspected already, that his double is himself. As he steps up to a large mirror, 'in extremity of terror, mine own image, but with features all pale and dabbled in blood, advanced to meet me with a feeble and tottering gait.' It is the other Wilson, but he no longer speaks in a whisper ... 'I could have fancied that I myself was speaking while he said: "You have conquered, and I yield. Yet henceforward art thou also dead ... In me didst thou exist — and, in my death, see by this image, which is thine own, how utterly thou hast murdered thyself."'

For the other Wilson was his conscience, trying to protect him from himself.

*The Man of the Crowd* is a lesser known story, but one of Poe's most haunting. As he describes the crowds that pour down the London streets, you can almost *hear* them. Poe starts by admitting: 'There are some secrets which do not permit themselves to be told. Men die nightly in their beds, wringing the hands of ghostly confessors, and looking them piteously in the eyes — die with despair of heart and convulsion of throat, on account of the hideousness of mysteries which will not *suffer themselves* to be revealed.'

He is at the bow window of a London coffee-house, watching the crowds go by. Out of the mass of humanity, as night falls, he notices one man in particular — a decrepit old man, but with an expression that catches his attention instantly:

'I had now a good opportunity of examining his person. He was short in stature, very thin, and apparently very feeble. His clothes, generally, were filthy and ragged; but as he came, now and then within the strong glare of a lamp, I perceived that his linen, although dirty, was of a beautiful texture; and my vision deceived me, or, through a rent in a closely-buttoned and evidently second-handed *roquelaire* which enveloped him, I caught a glimpse both of a diamond and of a dagger. These observations heightened my curiosity, and I resolved to follow the stranger withersoever he should go.'

He follows him through the night, through the fog that hangs over the city. Tying a handkerchief round his mouth, he keeps on. He crosses and re-crosses his way, again and again. He retraces his footsteps. They reach the outskirts of London, they return. Near daybreak, the old man finds a Gin Palace and forces his way in, to continue his pacing backwards and forward inside, until the place closes for the night and he has to leave again.

The sun rises. Still the narrator follows him – 'Long and swiftly he fled, while I followed him in the wildest amazement . . .' At last he can stand it no longer. 'And, as the shades of the second evening came on, I grew wearied unto death, and stopping fully in front of the wanderer, gazed at him steadfastly in the face. He noticed me not, but resumed his solemn walk, while I, ceasing to follow, remained absorbed in contemplation. "This old man," I said at length, "is the type and genius of deep crime. He refuses to be alone. *He is the man of the crowd.*"'

He realises he will never learn what the old man has done – that his crime is so horrible he cannot bear to be alone but has to thrust himself into the crowd in the vain hope of escaping from his conscience. The crime is too terrible to be told.

*The Tell-Tale Heart* is as perfect as any short story ever written. It is Poe's masterpiece of horror.

It starts with deceptive quiet, which builds up to the tremendous climax when the narrator is showing the police around the room where he has buried a man under the floorboards. He imagines he hears the beating of his heart, growing louder – and louder.

> 'They heard! – they suspected! – they *knew!* – they were making a mockery of my horror! – this I thought, and this I think. But anything was better than this agony. Anything was more tolerable than this derision! I could bear those hypocritical smiles no longer! I felt that I must scream or die! and now – again! – hark! louder! louder! louder! *louder!*
>
> ' "Villains!" I shrieked, "dissemble no more! I admit the deed! tear up the planks! here, here! – it is the beating of his hideous heart!" '

Yet again, the weight of his guilt is too awful for the conscience to bear.

Edgar Allan Poe (1809–49) was pursued by disaster throughout his life – this is one reason why he was such a master of horror. He wrote as if he were looking over his shoulder at someone or something behind him.

He was born in Boston, Massachussetts, on 19th January, 1809. His mother, an English actress, died when he was only two. He was then adopted by a businessman called John Allan, but from the start there was a bitter rivalry between the boy and his wealthy but miserly foster father.

When Poe was six, the Allans moved to England, and he went to a school at Stoke Newington on the outskirts of London from 1818 to 1820. There is an echo of London life and his school in some of his later stories (see *William*

*Wilson* and *The Man of the Crowd*), but Poe was essentially American in outlook.

He later went to university, but Allan removed him because of his debts. As he was penniless, for Allan refused to help him and even cut him out of his will, Poe joined the army and reached the rank of Sergeant Major. He joined West Point, the famous military academy, but was dismissed later for breaking rules.

In 1836 he made a startling marriage with his cousin Virginia – she was thirteen. Only six years later she broke a blood vessel when she was singing. She died in January 1847. In contrast to his child bride, he now proposed to several elderly women, but his life was rapidly falling to pieces. By 1849 he was terrified of going mad. In September that year he took a boat to Baltimore to make arrangements for his forthcoming marriage to a widow, Mrs Royster Shelton, who had some money and might have been able to look after him, but he vanished. A week later, his doctor received a note to come and fetch him, and found Poe unconscious and dressed in clothes that did not belong to him. No one knew what had happened. He was taken to hospital where he talked to 'spectral and imaginary objects on the walls'. On 7th October he cried out 'God help my poor soul,' and died. He was forty.

All his life Poe had been short of money, for his work was not popular. When some of his stories were published in two volumes as *Tales of the Grotesque and Arabesque*, his only payment was some free copies. When a friend visited him as his wife lay dying, he noted that: 'There was no clothing on the bed . . . the weather was cold and the sick lady had the dreadful chills that accompany the hectic fever of consumption. She lay on the straw bed, wrapped in her husband's greatcoat, with a large tortoise-shell cat on her bosom. The wonderful cat seemed conscious of her great usefulness. The coat and the cat were the sufferer's only means of warmth.' They could not afford to buy coal.

Poe tried to find escape by losing himself in drink, but when he came to himself again, his guilt was all the greater. Fortunately for us, he found escape in words as well. He used his private nightmares as the inspiration for his tales of horror. Sadly, he had little need to exaggerate – his own life was just as horrible.

## The Strange Case of Dr Jekyll and Mr Hyde

Robert Louis Stevenson (1850–94) owed a lot to Poe and was the first to admit it, praising him not only for the 'loathing and horror' in his work, but also for the 'almost incredible insight into the debatable region between sanity and madness.'

Like Poe he was possessed by a guilty conscience – but with a vital difference. Poe's *William Wilson* murders his conscience, but Stevenson's *Markheim* listens to it. *Markheim* was offered to the *Pall Mall Gazette* as their Christmas story in 1884, but was turned down as too short. Stevenson then submitted *The Body-Snatcher*, which he had written three years earlier but had put aside 'in a justifiable disgust, the tale being horrid.' But the *Pall Mall* editor was delighted and the story was advertised by sandwich-men carrying posters which the police suppressed because they were too lurid. Stevenson disliked the story so much that he refused to accept his fee of £40 – 'I was not able to produce my best; and I will be damned if I steal with my eyes open.' How many authors would be so modest today!

His liking for *Markheim* may have been personal rather than artistic, for it is a story of a man's conscience. The man Markheim visits an elderly antique dealer on Christmas

Day, to buy a present for a lady he is seeing that night. He starts back angrily when the dealer produces an antique looking-glass, crying: '... you give me this – this damned reminder of years, and sins and follies – this hand-conscience!'

As the old man fumbles about for something else, Markheim leaps on him from behind and stabs him to death. As he searches the shop for the dealer's hidden money, a stranger comes into the room. In the wavering candlelight, Markheim thinks he recognises him: '... he bore a likeness to himself; and always, like a lump of living terror, there lay in his bosom the conviction that this thing was not of the earth and not of God.'

He knows Markheim is looking for money and offers to tell him where it is, but the latter refuses angrily: 'I will take nothing at your hands; if I were dying of thirst, and it was your hand that put the pitcher to my lips, I should find the courage to refuse. It may be credulous, but I will do nothing to commit myself to evil.' The stranger also knows that Markheim wants the money to use on the Stock Exchange, and tells him that he will lose everything. He reminds him that only a few years before Markheim was a deeply religious man, and at last the latter repents. He rejects the stranger's suggestion that he should ransack the house and murder the maid, who has just returned unexpectedly – 'I have still my hatred of evil; and from that, to your galling disappointment, you shall see that I can draw both energy and courage.'

Now the visitor reveals his true nature, as Markheim's good conscience: 'The features of the visitor began to undergo a wonderful and lovely change: they brightened and softened with a tender triumph ...' He disappears. The bell rings again and Markheim answers the door to the maid. 'You had better go for the police,' he says. 'I have killed your master.'

Two years later Stevenson published his masterpiece of horror, *Dr Jekyll and Mr Hyde*, which had a similar theme. In spite of constant illness – or perhaps because of it, as if he knew that time was running out – Stevenson worked amazingly hard. *The Strange Case of Dr Jekyll and Mr Hyde* was written, rewritten and printed as a 'shilling shocker' within ten weeks.

It all started, or so Stevenson claimed, with a nightmare he had at the very time when he was searching desperately for a new plot. He started writing it down immediately. After three days he had finished 27,000 words. He read the manuscript to his wife Fanny, who did not like it. She said he had sacrificed a fine moral story to a 'magnificent piece of sensationalism'. After a fierce argument, Stevenson stalked up to his bedroom, where he had second thoughts. When he came down, he announced: 'You are right! I have absolutely missed the allegory, which, after all is the whole point of it – the very essence of it!' and he threw the pages on the fire to avoid the temptation of revising them. He started again from scratch and after a further three days completed the book.

Unlike *Markheim*, which seems artificial by comparison, *Jekyll* grips from the opening page. It starts with a conversation between two old friends – Mr Utterson, a lawyer, and Mr Enfield, a 'man about town'. As they pass the back door of an imposing house, on one of their evening walks, Enfield recalls an unpleasant incident he witnessed one night when he saw two figures ahead of him at this same spot, a short man and a young girl who was running along the pavement and bumped into him: '... then came the horrible part of the thing; for the man trampled calmly over the child's body and left her screaming on the ground. It sounds like nothing to hear, but it was hellish to see.'

Enfield had collared the man and an angry crowd gathered around them, including the child's parents. In order to quieten them, the man went inside the house by the back door and came out a few moments later with a cheque for £100 signed by someone else's name, a name that was highly respected. Enfield reveals the identity of the short man to Utterson – a Mr Hyde – and remarks: 'He is not easy to describe. There is something wrong with his appearance; something displeasing, something downright detestable. I never saw a man I so disliked, and yet I scarce know why. He must be deformed somewhere; he gives a strong feeling of deformity, although I couldn't specify the point. He's an extraordinary looking man, and yet I really can name nothing out of the way.'

Utterson is deeply disturbed. Hyde's name is all too familiar, for his old friend Dr Jekyll had revised his will a few weeks earlier with the strange condition that 'in case of Dr Jekyll's "disappearance or unexplained absence for any period exceeding three calendar months," the said Edward Hyde should step into the said Henry Jekyll's shoes without further delay . . .'

Utterson is now convinced that Jekyll is somehow under the influence of the evil Mr Hyde. He waits to confront Hyde and learn more about him. At last he sees him heading towards the back door of Jekyll's home. Hyde shrinks back as the lawyer touches him on the shoulder, but at least Utterson now knows what he looks like:

'Mr Hyde was pale and dwarfish . . . he had a displeasing smile . . . and he spoke with a husky, whispering and somewhat broken voice . . . but not all of these together could explain the hitherto unknown disgust, loathing and fear with which Mr Utterson regarded him. "There must be something else," said the perplexed gentleman. "There *is* something more, if I could find a name for it. God bless me, the man seems hardly human! Something troglodytic, shall we say? ... O my poor old Harry Jekyll, if ever I read Satan's signature upon a face, it is on that of your new friend." '

As the lawyer returns home, he thinks about Jekyll and gives the reader a hint that the doctor was not always as respectable as he seems: 'He was wild when he was young ... Ay, it must be that; the ghost of some old sin, the cancer of some concealed disgrace ...' Finally, he sees Jekyll and tells him outright that he has been learning about his new friend, Hyde, and does not like what he has heard. Jekyll refuses to discuss Hyde, but makes a promise: 'I will tell you one thing: the moment I choose, I can be rid of Mr Hyde. I give you my hand upon that ...' and he asks the lawyer to be tolerant. 'I have really a very great interest in poor Hyde ... I only ask you to help him for my sake, when I am no longer here.'

A year passes, and a maid is looking from her upstairs window when she sees a fine white-haired man below, and another smaller man coming towards him whom she recognises as Mr Hyde:

'He had in his hand a heavy cane, with which he was trifling ... all of a sudden he broke out in a great flame of anger, stamping with his foot, brandishing the cane, and carrying on (as the maid described it) like a madman. The old gentleman took a step back, with the air of one very much surprised and a trifle hurt; and at that Mr Hyde broke out of all bounds and clubbed him to the earth. And next moment, with ape-like fury, he was trampling his victim under foot, and hailing down a storm of blows, under which the bones were audibly shattered and the body jumped upon the roadway. At the horror of these sights and sounds, the maid fainted.'

Hyde flees to his lodgings in Soho, and when Jekyll is confronted by Utterson with his friend's crime he vows he will never see Hyde again: 'I am done with him in this world. It is all at an end.' But this is not so easy – Hyde is starting to take over. One morning Jekyll wakes up to discover that the hand resting on the bedclothes is that of Hyde – they are, of course, one and the same person. Sending a desperate message to his friend Dr Lanyon, to get the vital powders which he must take to change him back, Hyde becomes Jekyll before Lanyon's incredulous eyes. This is the famous transformation which haunts the reader's imagination afterwards in the same way as Frankenstein's Monster coming to life or Dracula emerging from his coffin:

'He put the glass to his lips and drank at one gulp. A cry followed; he reeled, staggered, clutched at the table and held on, staring with injected eyes, gasping with open mouth; and as I looked there came, I thought, a change – he seemed to swell – his face became suddenly black and the features seemed to melt and alter – and the next moment, I had sprung to my feet and leaped back against the wall, my arm raised to shield me from that prodigy, my mind submerged in terror.

"Oh God!" I screamed, and "Oh God!" again and again; for there before my eyes – pale and shaken, and half-fainting, and groping before him with his hands, like a man restored from death – there stood Henry Jekyll.'

The climax of the book is reached when the powders no longer work, and Hyde is unable to change back into Jekyll. He cowers in the back room, slipping notes under the door to his anxious butler Poole, who believes that his master has been murdered. Together with Utterson, Poole breaks down the door, but they are too late. Hyde lies there in Jekyll's clothes – he has taken his life. So, in a way, evil has destroyed itself.

The story ends with a statement left by Dr Jekyll and his explanation of Hyde, his double:

'It was on the moral side, and in my own person, that I learned to recognise the thorough and primitive duality of man . . . and from an early date, even before the course of my scientific discoveries had begun to suggest the most naked possibility of such a miracle, I had learned to dwell with pleasure, as a beloved daydream, on the thought of the separation of these elements. If each, I told myself, could but be housed in separate identities, life would be relieved of all that was unbearable: the unjust might go his way, delivered from the aspirations and remorse of his more upright twin; and the just could walk steadfastly and securely on his upward path.'

Once he has invented the potion which will change him into Hyde he discovers that the darker side of his nature is stronger than he has realised. He describes his feelings on drinking the potion:

> 'The most racking pangs succeeded: a grinding in the bones, deadly nausea, and a horror of the spirit that cannot be exceeded at the hour of birth or death. These agonies began swiftly to subside, and I came to myself as if out of a great sickness. There was something strange in my sensations, something indescribably new and, from its very novelty, incredibly sweet. I felt younger, lighter, happier in body; within I was conscious of a heady recklessness, a current of disordered sensual images running like a mill race in my fancy, a solution of the bonds of obligation, an unknown but not an innocent freedom of the soul. I knew myself, at the first breath of this new life, to be more wicked, tenfold more wicked, sold a slave to my original evil; and the thought, in that moment, braced and delighted me like wine.'

The reader, too, has a sneaking sympathy for Hyde, who is much more *fun* than the virtuous Jekyll. At least he is a complete person in his villainy, whereas Jekyll suffers from a lifetime of suppressing the natural instincts he enjoyed as a young man, and pays dearly for his pretence of perfection. Through him, Stevenson attacks the Victorian hypocrisy of men who seemed the height of respectability – ideal husbands and fond fathers – but in fact led double lives. Jekyll is in fact as guilty as Hyde. It is a moral story, and the moral can be summed up like this: never try to be someone else; accept yourself as you are, faults and all.

It is generally accepted that Stevenson's *The Strange Case* of *Dr Jekyll and Mr Hyde* was inspired by a dream, but it is more likely that he drew on personal experience to write the novel, for Stevenson was a Jekyll and Hyde in real life, and tormented by his conscience.

He was born in Edinburgh in 1850 and his family was highly respectable. However, his father encouraged Robert's writing, and paid for the publication of one of his 'blood-and-thunder' stories when he was only sixteen. At seventeen, Robert joined the Engineering Department of Edinburgh University, where he was considered rather an eccentric.

Many people tolerated him simply because of his respectable background, but this was the one thing he could not tolerate himself. He did not understand his parents and complained that they did not understand him: 'I never feel so lonely as when I am too much with my father and mother, and I am ashamed of the feelings, which makes matters worse.' Here was the first sign of guilt that was to leap out later in such stories as *Markheim* and *Dr Jekyll*.

To the dismay of his family, he abandoned engineering and found his escape in the back streets of Edinburgh, fascinated by the smoke and squalor of waterfront pubs and the 'dregs of humanity' he found there – all of it invaluable material for his writing. Standards were different then and respectable society pretended that such places and such people did not exist – Stevenson was forced to lead a double life. This could have been a passing phase, easily forgotten, but then he suddenly fell in love with a beautiful young girl called Kate Drummond. They were attracted to each other immediately and planned to marry, but his father was so shocked that he threatened the worst punishment he could think of – to stop Robert's allowance of £12 a year. Stevenson surrendered and, in doing so, condemned Kate to a life of squalor. He never forgave himself.

Now he had to conform and abandon the zest of rebellion. But he went on to write such classics as *Treasure Island* and *Kidnapped*, and released some of his guilt in horror stories such as *Dr Jekyll*.

When he was twenty-six he married Fanny Osbourne. She was thirty-six, with a daughter of seventeen and a son of eight by a previous marriage. A greater contrast to the unfortunate Kate could hardly be imagined, but his family accepted her as the lesser of two evils even though she was 'grizzled' in appearance and a grandmother. Fanny nursed Stevenson through his constant illness from tuberculosis, but also censored his writing. When he wrote a romantic novel with a heroine based on Kate Drummond, she destroyed the manuscript. After that, he seldom included women in his writing. 'My wife hates and loathes and slates my women,' he wrote to his closest friend. Some of the books he wanted to write would have shocked the public he was gaining and might have been banned by libraries, so she was right to dissuade him, but at the same time, she stopped him from stretching his vivid imagination to the utmost – she tamed his genius.

On his father's death, they moved to America and the healthy mountain air of Colorado. But tuberculosis was hard to cure in those days and Stevenson remained wretchedly ill. He spent the £3000 left him in buying a yacht and sailing it to Samoa where he bought 300 acres and made a new home. He became known to the natives as *Tusitala*, the teller of tales, but in England he was referred to as 'The King of the Cannibal Islands'. He was hard at work on the *Weir of Hermiston* when he died on 3rd December, 1894, aged forty-four.

## The Picture of Dorian Gray

Here is another example of the 'double' in literature. Written by Oscar Wilde in 1891, it is witty and elegant, and even if it is not a true 'horror story', the theme is horrific.

Basil Hallward paints a portrait of his friend Dorian Gray – an exceptionally good-looking young man. When Gray sees it he exclaims: 'Why should it keep what I must lose? Every moment that passes takes something from me, and gives something to it. Oh, if it were only the other way! If the picture could change, and I could be always what I am now!' His wish is granted. As his own private life becomes increasingly vile, he looks as young and handsome as ever. But his portrait, locked away in an upstairs room, changes and becomes hideously evil.

After he has murdered Hallward and the portrait has become crueller than ever, Gray decides to destroy it: 'There was only one bit of evidence left against him. The picture itself – that was evidence . . . Once it had given him pleasure to watch it changing and growing old. Of late he had felt no such pleasure . . . It had been like a conscience to him . . . He would destroy it.'

He slashes the portrait with the murder weapon. The servants hear a terrible scream and a crash. They break in: 'When they entered they found, hanging upon the wall, a splendid portrait of their master as they had last seen him, in all the wonder of his exquisite youth and beauty. Lying on the floor was a dead man, in evening dress, with a knife in his heart. He was withered, wrinkled and loathsome of visage. It was not till they had examined the rings that they recognised who it was.'

## Dracula

Written by Bram Stoker, this novel was published in 1897.

The story takes the form of entries from a certain Jonathan Harker's journal. He is a young solicitor travelling across Europe towards Castle Dracula in Transylvania. Count Dracula is interested in buying a house outside London and Harker has brought the documents of a place that seems suitable, called Carfax.

The opening of Stoker's novel is magnificent. Arriving at the old fashioned Golden Krone Hotel in Bistritz, Harker finds a letter waiting for him from the count: 'MY FRIEND – Welcome to the Carpathians ... At the Borgo Pass my carriage will await you and will bring you to me. I trust that your journey from London has been a happy one and that you will enjoy your stay in my beautiful land. Your friend, Dracula.' It might have been more appropriate if Dracula had signed himself 'Your fiend' rather than 'Your friend', but Harker has no suspicion of danger until the following morning when the landlord's wife implores him not to go. She explains that this is the eve of St George's Day, and that 'when the clock strikes midnight, all the evil things in the world will have full sway.' She begs him to take the crucifix she wears – 'for your mother's sake' – and ties it round his neck.

A crowd has gathered around the carriage outside, and Harker notices that the people cross themselves and point two fingers towards him. A fellow passenger explains that this is a sign to ward off the evil eye.

The carriage reaches the Borgo Pass an hour before midnight, but there is no one waiting to take Harker to Castle Dracula. The driver urges him to continue and return the next day, but the horses begin to snort and plunge wildly while he is speaking. A carriage suddenly appears, driven by a tall man with a long brown beard and a great black hat which hides his face.

## The Beaver Book of Horror

Harker's luggage is transferred, and he continues his journey. After a while he notices a flickering blue flame in the distance. The driver stops and disappears into the darkness, and Harker finds the carriage surrounded by wolves. When the driver returns, they vanish. They arrive at the castle, and the door is opened by the count:

> 'Within stood a tall old man, clean-shaven save for a long white moustache, and clad in black from head to foot, without a single speck of colour about him anywhere ... The old man motioned me in with his right hand with a courtly gesture, saying in excellent English, but with a strange intonation: *"Welcome to my house! Enter freely and of your own will!"*'

His hand clasp is very strong and as cold as ice – 'more like the hand of a dead than living man'. Inside Castle Dracula, it is not as bleak as you might imagine. Far from it – the curtains and furniture are so lavish they remind Harker of Hampton Court.

As he enjoys his meal, Harker studies the count: 'The mouth, so far as I could see it under the heavy moustache, was fixed and rather cruel-looking, with peculiarly sharp teeth; these protruded over the lips, whose remarkable ruddiness showed astonishing vitality in a man of his years.' When the count leans over him, he notices the hairs on the palms of his hands and his finger-nails cut to sharp points. By now it is nearly dawn, and he shows Harker to his bedroom – 'I have to be away till the afternoon; so sleep well and dream well!' He bows courteously and leaves.

Harker sleeps late after his journey, and finds his breakfast waiting for him after he has dressed. As he explores the rooms he is greatly impressed by all the treasures, though he is surprised there is no servant in sight and not a single mirror anywhere.

When the count returns they get down to business, and Harker gives him the necessary papers to sign for the house he is buying. As he describes the gloominess of the place – the dark pool, barred windows, derelict chapel and a private lunatic asylum nearby – Count Dracula seems delighted. Again they talk till dawn, when the count jumps up, excuses himself and leaves.

Next something happens to make Harker feel 'there is something so strange about this place and all in it that I cannot but feel uneasy.' He has started to shave one morning, using his own small shaving-glass, when he is startled to feel a hand on his shoulder and hear the count say good morning: '... it amazed me that I had not seen him, since the reflection of the whole glass covered the whole room behind me.' Turning to the glass again, he realises there is no reflection – the count is beside him but cannot be seen in the glass. In his surprise, Harker cuts himself slightly and realises that blood is trickling down his chin. 'I laid down the razor ... When the count saw my face, his eyes blazed with a sort of demoniac fury, and he suddenly made a grab at my throat. I drew away, and his hand touched the string of beads which held the crucifix. It made an instant change in him, for the fury passed so quickly that I could hardly believe that it was ever there.' 'Take care,' warns the count, 'it is more dangerous than you think in this country.' He seizes the glass and throws it out of the window. It shatters into a thousand pieces on the stones of the courtyard far below. The count leaves, and Harker simply records that 'it is very annoying, for I do not see how I am to shave'. He uses the lid of his watch case instead.

That day, Harker discovers that all the doors in the castle are locked, and he is a prisoner. A night or two later, all of his fears are realised as he looks out of his bedroom window and notices something below:

> 'What I saw was the count's head coming out from the window. I did not see the face, but I knew the man by the neck and the movement of his back and arms. In any case, I could not mistake the hands which I had so many opportunities of studying. I was at first interested and somewhat amused, for it is wonderful how small a matter will interest and amuse a man when he is a prisoner. But my very feelings changed to repulsion and terror when I saw the whole man slowly emerge from the window and begin to crawl down the castle wall over that dreadful abyss, *face down*, with his cloak spreading out around him like great wings.'

In fact, Jonathan Harker is not alone in Castle Dracula. He discovers this when he finds an unlocked door leading to an empty room, where he falls asleep. When he wakes up, three young women are bending over him. At first he thinks he is dreaming, for they are standing in the moonlight but throw no shadow. Then one of the girls fastens her teeth on to his neck, and at this moment Count Dracula bursts into the room. He sweeps the girl aside, shouting: 'How dare you touch him, any of you? How dare you cast eyes on him when I had forbidden it?'

'Are we to have nothing tonight?' one of them asks, and he nods towards a bag he has thrown on the floor. Harker thinks he hears the wail of a half-smothered child, and sinks back unconscious.

Later, looking out of his bedroom window, he sees the count climbing like a lizard down the walls, wearing Harker's own clothes. His terrible bag is slung over his shoulder, and Harker suspects Dracula is trying to convince the local peasants that he is the one guilty of seizing their children. Sure enough, it is not long before a woman in the courtyard below looks up and shouts: 'Monster, give me my child!' when she sees his face at the window. The count calls up a pack of wolves, who tear her to pieces.

Trying to escape, Harker enters the cellars of the castle and finds boxes full of earth in one of the vaults. The count is lying inside one of them and seems to be dead, but comes to him the next day to announce his farewell: 'Tomorrow, my friend, we must part. You return to your beautiful England, I to some work which may have such an end that we may never meet.' By now, Harker realises that Dracula has no intention of letting him leave the castle alive and has tricked him into writing letters home saying he has left already. So he makes one final attempt to flee the castle and returns to the vault. He raises the lid of the box in which the count is lying:

> 'I saw something which filled my very soul with horror. There lay the count, but looking as if his youth had been half-renewed, for the white hair and moustache were changed to dark-iron grey; the cheeks were fuller, and the white skin seemed ruby-red underneath; the mouth was redder than ever, for on the lips were gouts of fresh blood, which trickled from the corners of the mouth and ran over the chin and neck. Even the deep burning eyes seemed set amongst swollen flesh, for the lids and pouches underneath were bloated. It seemed as if the whole

awful creature were simply gorged with blood; he lay like a filthy leech, exhausted with repletion.'

He picks up a shovel and brings the edge down on to the count's face, but the head turns and the eyes fasten on Harker 'with all their blaze of basilisk horror' so that he falters and his blow leaves only a gash on the count's forehead.

This is a good place to break off and urge you to read the original novel by Bram Stoker for yourself. There is plenty of excitement ahead, so read on and find out for yourself.

Why did Bram Stoker write *Dracula*? There are several theories. The most popular is that the idea for the story came to Stoker in a dream, in the same way that Mary Shelley's dream gave her the idea for *Frankenstein* – it is believed that Stoker dined too well on dressed crab and had a nightmare.

The Dracula Society claims that Stoker based the count on the historical Dracula – Vlad the Impaler (see Chapter 8). Certainly he used historical information as background material, and this is how he stumbled on the name. He had the flair to realise what a wonderful title it would make – *Drac-ula* – it echoes as you say it! – the only one of his books which uses a single word for the title. But there is no reason to suspect that Vlad was a vampire or even thought of as such.

Many other theories have been proposed, but it could be that all the distinguished professors are looking for something that is not there, and that in writing *Dracula*, Stoker had a rattling good story to tell and simply wanted to tell it.

## Horror Stories

Bram Stoker had two sides to his personality. Outwardly he was strong and stalwart, but inwardly he was unsure of himself, and had a particular obsession with the strange and the supernatural. He developed this craving when he was a boy, confined to his bed for the first eight years of his life with an illness which has never been explained. To entertain him, his mother Charlotte told him stories of the terrible cholera epidemic that swept across Europe to Western Ireland where she lived with her family when she was a girl. Odd stories for a sickly child, about people buried alive (see Chapter 2), but they made a deep impression on Bram.

After leaving Trinity College, Dublin, Bram followed his father, Abraham, into the Irish Civil Service. To escape from the monotony of his job, he wrote a serial called *The Chain of Destiny*, about a character called 'the phantom of the fiend', for the *Shamrock* magazine, and reviewed plays for the *Dublin Mail* in return for a free seat in the theatre.

This was how he met the young English actor, Henry Irving. The two soon became great friends, and when Irving asked Stoker to join him in London a couple of years later after he had bought the Lyceum Theatre, he did not hesitate. He chucked up his safe career in the Civil Service, married Florence Balcombe and sailed for England. His mother commented scornfully: 'He has gone as Manager to a strolling player.'

But Stoker's devotion was rewarded. Irving triumphed at the Lyceum and he was able to bask in the actor's reflected glory, meeting all the important 'lions' of the day. All the time he was writing – he wrote eighteen books altogether – and sometimes he managed to holiday on his own, striding across the countryside as if he had a surplus of energy. On a walking tour in Scotland, he stumbled on the small fishing village of Cruden Bay, and it was here that he wrote his masterpiece *Dracula*.

There had been many books on vampires, but Stoker skimmed the cream of all the best vampire legends and brought them up to date. A Hungarian university professor told him of superstitions in that part of the world and the belief that vampires existed in Transylvania across the Hungarian border, and it seems certain that he also told Stoker of the real 'Dracula' – a man of extraordinary cruelty (see Chapter 8). With the help of an old guidebook and the library in the British Museum, Stoker's vivid imagination did the rest.

His genius was to place *Dracula* in the setting of contemporary Victorian England. This made the story seem close to home and possible, just as Alfred Hitchcock traps an ordinary man in his films and plunges him into an extraordinary situation. In *Dracula*, Stoker refers to contemporary newspaper reports, Kodak snaps and even an early version of the tape-recorder. Consequently, the fantastic figure of Count Dracula seems more real.

The book was published in 1897. It had a mixed reception, but the most prophetic comment came from his mother Charlotte: 'My dear it is splendid, a thousand miles beyond anything you have written before, and I feel certain will place you very high in the writers of the day ... No book since Mrs Shelley's *Frankenstein* or indeed any other at all has come near yours in originality, or terror – Poe is nowhere. I have read much but I have never met a book like it at all. In its terrible excitement it should make a widespread reputation and much money for you.'

This was true of the distant future, but sadly wrong as far as Stoker was concerned. *Dracula* has made a fortune for others. It has become an industry with Dracula kites,

Dracula lollies and fangs that go crunch in the night, but Stoker never enjoyed national fame or fortune.

When Henry Irving became the first actor to be honoured with a knighthood, the tide had already started to turn against him. Bad health, a fire that destroyed the warehouse with all the Lyceum's scenery, and the failure of several costly productions led to the loss of his theatre and his collapse and death in October 1905. It had been a great friendship and Stoker was desolate. He suffered a slight stroke and from then on had to write with the help of a magnifying glass. His last novel, *The Lair of the White Worm* (see Chapter 6), is one of the weirdest books ever written and suggests that he was deeply disturbed.

He died in poverty on 20th April, 1912, at the age of sixty-four, and was buried at Golders Green in London. Unhonoured in his lifetime and barely mentioned in encyclopaedias, Bram Stoker has been the least known author of one of the best known books ever written – until now. At long last he is recognised as a great writer, and the Greater London Council have announced that they will honour his memory with a commemorative blue plaque to mark the house where he lived in London.

### The Phantom of the Opera

Like most of these horror stories, the original novel by Gaston Leroux published in 1911 is more weird than any of the familiar film versions.

In his prologue the author claims that this is a true story. It concerns the masked Ghost who haunts the Opera House in Paris. There are numerous cellars and passages in the Opera House – a honeycomb of a place where the phantom can disappear and reappear miraculously, rather like the Hunchback who haunted the ramparts of Notre Dame, but occasionally he is glimpsed as he scurries away. The Ghost's voice is heard everywhere. Eventually it is revealed that in his lifetime he was a brilliant ventriloquist, and his name is Erik. In one of the most dramatic scenes in the novel Carlotta, the great star of the French opera, appears on stage. The Ghost has threatened that a catastrophe will take place. It does! Suddenly her marvellous voice is transformed into the hideous croak of a toad. The Ghost then brings the huge chandelier down on to the audience, but only one person is killed – a country woman who had come to the Opera for the first time in her life.

The two managers of the Opera are new to the job and unable at first to accept all the wild rumours concerning the Ghost. When they receive his demand for 240,000 francs a year and Box number 5 to be placed at his disposal, they think they are the victims of a practical joke. But as further disasters occur and people disappear or are found dead, they begin to wonder. So does the reader: at this stage the story is more a 'whatisit?' than a 'whodunnit?'

On one level the book is a romance, because the Opera Ghost is in love with Christine Daae, a young, not very talented singer. With his own musical genius, he manages to inspire her, and the first time that the star Carlotta falls ill, Christine replaces her and triumphs. Unfortunately, the handsome young Vicomte de Chagny, Raoul, is in love with her too. The Ghost's jealousy is inflamed and finally he traps Christine in his underground lair. Later, she tells Raoul how she unmasked the Ghost, and here there are echoes from the age-old story of Beauty and the Beast:

'If I lived to be a hundred, I should always hear the superhuman cry of grief and rage which he uttered when the terrible sight appeared before my eyes ...

imagine, if you can, Red Death's mask suddenly coming to life in order to express, with the four black holes of its eyes, its nose, and its mouth, the extreme anger, the mighty fury of a demon; *and not a ray of light except from the sockets*, for, as I learned later, you can not see his blazing eyes except in the dark.'

He seizes her hands and digs them into his face, tearing his terrible dead flesh with her nails, and shouting: 'Know that I am built up of death from head to foot and that it is a corpse that loves you and adores you and will never, never leave you! ... Look, I am not laughing now, I am crying, crying for you Christine, who have torn off my mask and who therefore can never leave me again!' Gaining his trust, Christine is released by the Ghost on the understanding that she will return, but when he overhears her plan to escape from Paris with Raoul, he imprisons her again – to live with him forever, or die.

There is much in the book that does not stand too close an examination. Even though the Ghost wears a pasteboard nose with a moustache attached to it, the ease with which he travels outside the Opera House is never explained. Some parts of the book are silly, but it is the *idea* that is so tremendous. At the end, the Ghost allows the two lovers to leave, realising that Christine feels pity for him and not the love he craves.

### Sheridan Le Fanu (1814–73)

Le Fanu has been hailed as 'a master of mystery and horror', and many people have compared him to Poe. He was brilliant in hinting at horror rather than stating it, yet he is still underrated and not as well known as he should be. This is possibly because there is no single masterpiece, like *Dracula* in the case of Bram Stoker, to make him famous, but several outstanding stories such as *Carmilla* and *Green Tea*. He started writing late in life, when he was nearing fifty, but made up for this by producing twelve books in his last twelve years.

Le Fanu sounds a French name and it came from his Huguenot family which settled in Dublin in the eighteenth century, but he was as Irish as his young fellow Dubliner, Bram Stoker, on whom he had a profound influence.

His description of the destruction of the female vampire in *Carmilla* was written twenty-five years before *Dracula*, but when you read Stoker's novel you will see how it lingered in imagination –

> 'The body, therefore, in accordance with the ancient practice, was raised, and a sharp stake driven through the heart of the vampire, who uttered a piercing shriek at the moment, in all respects such as might escape from a living person in the last agony. Then the head was struck off, and a torrent of blood flowed from the severed neck. The body and head were next placed on a pile of wood, and reduced to ashes, which were thrown upon the river and borne away, and that territory has never since been plagued by visits of a vampire.'

*Green Tea* is the story of Mr Jennings – a clergyman haunted by the evil presence of a small black monkey, visible only to himself, even when his eyes are shut. At last it gains too great a control and the clergyman kills himself, leaving a note for the doctor who has been trying to help him:

'Dear Dr Hesselius. – It is here. You had not been an hour gone when it returned. It is speaking. It knows all that has happened. It knows everything – it knows you, and is frantic and atrocious. It reviles. I send you this. It knows every word I have written – I write this. This I promised, and therefore write, but I fear very confused, very incoherently. I am so interrupted, disturbed.'

This is, of course, another tale of conscience (apart from the possible hallucinatory effect of a drug – the 'green tea' – on Mr Jennings). It could be that in the clergyman's past there was something so terrible that he could not endure living with it. With real murderers, guilt often takes the form of anonymous letters accusing themselves; with Mr Jennings, it was a little black monkey on his back.

## Ambrose Bierce (1842–1914?)

An American journalist and writer of short stories, Bierce is considered one of the masters of horror. When he was a young man he enlisted in the Union Army to fight in the American Civil War, and many of the things he witnessed – such as wild pigs eating the corpses of soldiers – were described in *Tales of Soldiers and Civilians*, published in San Francisco in 1891. His preface revealed that it was published by a friend – 'Denied existence by the chief publishing houses of this country' – but it was more successful in England, his home for four years, where it was called *In the Midst of Life*.

Bierce was a bitter man, and released his venom in a famous newspaper column called *The Prattler*, which he wrote for many years. Another work, his *Devil's Dictionary*, included such sour definitions as this one, for *Handkerchief*:

'a small square of silk or linen used at funerals to conceal a lack of tears'.

Bierce's most famous horror stories were published in *Can Such Things Be?* (1893). He resented the lack of recognition he received at the time, but the stories are admired today as classics of horror. He *enjoyed* horror – when he was accused of frightening his readers, he replied: 'If it scares you to read that one imaginary person killed another, why not take up knitting.' The stories include *Moxon's Master*, an early variation on the Frankenstein theme, about a machine which develops powers of thought and runs amok when it loses a game of chess, and *The Death of Halpin Frayser*, which starts with this tremendous paragraph:

> 'One dark night in midsummer a man waking from a dreamless sleep in a forest lifted his head from the earth, and staring a few moments into the blackness, said: "Catherine Larue". He said nothing more; no reason was known to him why he should have said so much.'

He finds a shallow pool and plunges his hand into it:

> 'It stained his fingers; it was blood! Blood, he then observed, was about him everywhere. The weeds growing rankly by the roadside showed it in blots and splashes on their big, broad leaves. Patches of dry dust between the wheelways were pitted and spattered as with a red rain. Defiling the trunks of trees were broad maculations of crimson, and blood dripped like dew from their foliage.'

He is attacked by a lunatic, and found by two men, horribly murdered.

Bierce had a powerful visual sense, and was proud also of his pure English style. He hated being compared to anyone else, especially Edgar Allan Poe. Poe's tales shriek with humanity – the one quality that Bierce lacks absolutely.

Perhaps the most extraordinary thing about Bierce's private life was his death – he disappeared off the face of the earth when he went to cover the civil war in Mexico. The truth of the end of 'Bitter Bierce', who 'set a level of viciousness and brutality seldom surpassed in American journalism', will never be known.

## M. R. James (1862–1936)

Dr Montague Rhodes James knew the power of suggestion – of what *might be* rather than what actually *is*. His ghost stories, which are beautifully written, offer no explanations – there is never a neat solution at the end.

*Oh, Whistle, and I'll Come to You My Lad* is one of James's most celebrated stories and concerns a bronze whistle from another age which, when blown, summons up 'a horrible, an intensely horrible face *of crumpled linen*'.

Considering how delicate James's stories are, they adapt to television surprisingly well. Both *Oh, Whistle . . .* and *Lost Hearts* have been filmed for the small screen, and the latter came across with special brilliance. A young boy is staying with his kindly cousin Mr Abney, when he is warned of danger by the ghosts of two children who have been murdered by him:

> 'Whilst the girl stood still, half smiling, with her hands clasped over her heart, the boy, a thin shape, with black hair and ragged clothing, raised his arms in the air with an appearance of menace and of unappeasable hunger and longing. The moon shone

upon his almost transparent hands, and Stephen saw that the nails were fearfully long and that the light shone through them. As he stood with his arms thus raised, he disclosed a terrifying spectacle. On the left side of his chest there opened a black and gaping rent; and there fell upon Stephen's brain, rather than upon his ear, the impression of one of those hungry and desolate cries that he had heard resounding over the woods of Aswarby all that evening. In another moment this dreadful pair had moved swiftly and noiselessly over the dry gravel, and he saw them no more.'

Had Stephen imagined this? No. Mr Abney is found dead, his left side torn open in a huge wound, exposing his heart.

In spite of his talent for writing stories full of menace, M. R. James was the least menacing of men – a Professor, former Provost of Eton, and Fellow of All Souls College, Cambridge. He wrote his stories in his spare time, the most famous being *Ghost Stories of an Antiquary* (1904). Did he believe in ghosts? 'I am prepared to consider evidence and accept it if it satisfies me.' This is as far as he was prepared to go. But he did permit himself this warning: 'Be careful how you handle the packet you pick up in the carriage-drive, particularly if it contains nail-parings and hair. Do not, in any case, bring it into the house; *it may not be alone.*'

# 5
# HORROR ON STAGE AND SCREEN

'*What would a man look like whose brain had been taken from the head of another man, "transplanted as it were"? How would a hand appear that had been "grafted" on to another arm? How would the eyes of a dead man appear if they were suddenly to open?*'

(Jack Pierce, make-up man, on his creation of Frankenstein's monster)

## Curtains for Dracula

Horror films often develop from stage versions of stories rather than directly from the novels themselves. The best known horror stories were adapted for the stage remarkably early – for instance *Frankenstein* was presented at the Adelphi Theatre, London, in 1850, with the title *Frankenstein, or The Model Man*, and *Jekyll and Hyde* was withdrawn from the Lyceum Theatre in 1888 out of respect to the public, already scared to death by the murders of Jack the Ripper. As for *Dracula*, it is claimed that a stage version is *always* in production somewhere in the world. The birth of *Dracula* on stage, and how this became involved with the cult of the Vamp in Hollywood, is a fascinating story.

It starts at ten in the morning on 18th May, 1897, at the great Lyceum Theatre off the Strand in London. Outside, a dark green poster announced the following performance in bold black letters: 'For the first time – A Drama – in prologue and five acts – DRACULA or the Un-Dead by Bram Stoker.' Inside the theatre, special programmes listed a staggering total of forty-seven scenes, such as 'Outside the Castle' or 'Outside the Tomb'. The cast list revealed that the part of Count Dracula was being taken by a man called Mr Jones – an actor who does not seem to have been heard of before or since.

Where was the audience? A few figures huddled in the auditorium, including Bram Stoker's cook. A closer look at the poster gives an explanation: the 'Admission' cost one guinea, a staggering price when you consider that the best seat in the Dress Circle that evening, to watch Sir Henry Irving in one of his great classical productions, cost only seven shillings (about 35 pence). Yet this was being shown at the undramatic hour of 10 a.m. What on earth was going on?

The answer is simple. *Dracula* had just been published that month and Bram Stoker plainly thought it was possible that his story might be adapted for the stage. But in those days, the ideas and titles of books were stolen – or 'pirated' – without the author's permission and without any payment. The best legal safeguard was the formality of *one* production on stage, complete with poster and programme, which would establish the author's copyright. This was what Stoker was doing, and as he was the Acting Manager of the Lyceum he was able to use his own theatre for the morning read-through. As for 'Admission One Guinea', that was deliberately to *discourage* the public. He did not want them to see it – nor did they.

One of the few people who did see the performance was the great actor Henry Irving himself. He was passing through the theatre when he heard the actors reading their lines on stage.

'What are they doing?' he is supposed to have asked.

'It's Stoker's vampire book. What do you think of it?'

'*DREADFUL!*' Apparently his famous voice boomed throughout the theatre and hurt Bram Stoker deeply. There was no chance of Irving playing Count Dracula, though he would have been ideal for the part! That, as far as Stoker knew, was that. *Dracula* was not produced in his lifetime, and the actor called Mr Jones sank into theatrical oblivion.

But a strange process had begun. 1897 was a good year for vampires. Stoker's book had already created an interest which was heightened by a controversial painting called *The Vampire*, shown in the summer exhibition of the New Gallery. Painted by a friend of Stoker's, Philip Burne-Jones, it portrayed a woman leaning over a bare-chested man. Blood trickled from punctures in his skin. It caused a sensation, and ladies and gentlemen of polite Victorian society flocked to the Gallery for a fashionable thrill. The programme accompanying the exhibition contained a poem written by a relative of the painter – Rudyard Kipling. This was also called *The Vampire*, and is magnificent – here are the first and fifth verses:

> *A Fool there was and he made his prayer*
> *(Even as you and I!)*
> *To a rag and a bone and a hank of hair*
> *(We called her the woman who did not care)*
> *But the fool he called her his lady fair*
> *(Even as you and I).*
>
> *The fool was stripped to his foolish hide*
> *(Even as you and I)*
> *Which she might have seen when she threw him aside –*
> *(But it isn't on record the lady tried)*
> *So some of him lived but the most of him died*
> *(Even as you and I).*

Life was more leisurely in those days. With no cinema or television it was possible for a single painting to become a 'celebrity'. *The Vampire* and the accompanying programme crossed the Atlantic and became a sensation in New York too. Public interest was so keen that a play was based on them, called *A Fool There Was*, and when this was presented on Broadway the film rights were bought up by a man called Fox, later to become world famous as Twentieth Century Fox.

Not only did Mr Fox wish to make a film – he decided to create the first film 'star' and chose a young actress called Theodosia Goodman. This name was not glamorous enough, so he changed it to Theda Bara which is an anagram of Arab Death.

Some people say this was just a coincidence, but in any case the publicity men seized their chance. The hint of Arabia was perfect for a film about a woman who treated men with contempt. Theda Bara was photographed leaning over a male skeleton, she wore bat-like capes, and it was claimed that she was born in the shade of the pyramids. She gave interviews, in broken English, in darkened hotel bedrooms reeking of incense. It has been said that when the newspapermen left, she would dash across the room, fling back the curtains and open the window with a cry of 'Gimme some air!'

But the publicity worked. Grateful for a good story, the press played along with the fantasy. Theda Bara was presented to the public as the first 'vamp' in the silent film *A Fool There Was*, which had the sub-title 'Kiss me my fool' – a line that was taken up by young film-goers. Vamps became the rage. The cult of the vamp or vampire had been established.

Meanwhile, back in England, the stage manager of a provincial repertory company (Jack Howarth, known to millions of television viewers as Albert Tatlock of *Coronation Street*) loaned his copy of *Dracula* to his producer, Hamilton Deane. Deane, an Irishman like Bram Stoker, was a 'matinee idol' of the English provinces. He sensed the potential success of *Dracula* on stage, bought the rights from Stoker's widow, and adapted it. For good measure he added a small part for Jack Howarth, as the warder. There was surprisingly little for Dracula to do – the occasional appearance and just a few lines, like his curious opening words to the maid: 'I have sorrow if I have given to you the alarm – perhaps my foot-fall sounds not so heavy as that of your English ploughman.' The part went to an actor called Edmund Blake.

*Dracula* opened at the Grand Theatre, Derby, in June 1924. Soon the company realised they had struck gold. Hamilton Deane decided to invade the West End of London, and when theatre managements turned him down scornfully he backed the production himself with the help of a Lancashire businessman. The play opened at the Little Theatre on 14th February, 1927. The critics deplored it. The public loved it, and the play ran for 391 performances.

Deane was an actor-manager of the old school, with a flair for dramatic effects. His script contained detailed instructions for the actor playing Dracula: 'Trousers must be strapped under feet – one foot to be secured inside window to solid rostrum. The Inverness Cape which he wears must be heavily wired, so that when face downwards, it assumes the shape of a Bat's Wings.' There were tricks with fake coffins full of earth, but as the inventor refused to allow anyone else to use them he had to be made up as Count Dracula as well, with a lot of wig and lifts in his shoes as he was very small! Above all, Deane thought of a brilliant 'gimmick' for his London production – a Red Cross nurse in the foyer, just in case someone collapsed from fright. One evening a man was feeling ill and left his seat in the stalls. As he did so, the lights dimmed on stage and he lost his balance, resting his hand on a woman in the row in front of him who was wearing a backless evening dress. She screamed, and both of them *did* faint!

Deane had given himself the best speech in the play, as he warns the others of the power of the vampire:

'He is Brute and more than Brute, and the heart of
him is not. He cannot die by mere passing of time.

So long as he can fatten on the blood of the living – he can grow younger. He can transform himself at will to any of the forms of meaner things: such as the rat – the bat – the wolf. He can come in mist which he creates, or in the moonlight rays as elemental dust. He can vanish at will. He can see in the dark. He can do all these things – yet he is not free. His power ceases, as does that of all evil things, at the coming of day – he can only change himself – at his change time – at Moon, or at exact Sunrise or Sunset.'

But his finest speech was made to the audience after the curtain had fallen. Deane advanced before the curtains:

'Just a moment, ladies and gentlemen! Just a word before you leave. We hope the memories of Dracula and Renfield won't give you bad dreams, so just a word of reassurance. When you get home tonight and the lights have been turned out and you are afraid to look behind the curtains and you dread to see a face appear at the window – why, just pull yourself together! And remember that after all THERE ARE SUCH THINGS!'

Hamilton Deane eventually became a victim of his own creation. *Dracula* was in such demand that gradually it replaced the other plays in his repertory. Audiences would not let him abandon it, but he was able to console himself: 'We never had a poor house with *Dracula* . . . I could not go wrong with it anywhere.' In 1939, he at last played the part of Count Dracula himself. Suitably, this production was presented at the Lyceum Theatre where the first read-through had taken place in 1897. There was an emotional moment one evening when Bela Lugosi, who was filming in England, walked on to the stage and embraced the other 'Dracula' as the audience cheered. Deane continued to tour the provinces with *Dracula* until 1941, when he made a last appearance at St Helen's in Lancashire. He died in 1958, just as Dracula was being resurrected by Hammer films and Christopher Lee.

## Horror film classics

This is a list of the author's own favourites.

*The Cabinet of Dr Caligari* (1919)

One of the earliest and greatest of all horror films. Made in Germany by Robert Wiene, it is the story of a series of murders carried out by a sleepwalker who is under the control of a mad doctor. It is weird even today, and the climax in the asylum, when you can hardly tell who is sane and who is not, is still horrifying.

*Nosferatu* (1922)

This is the first Dracula film. Another early German silent, it broke new ground by filming in real locations rather than the studio sets of Caligari. Friedrich Murnau, the director, made the silly mistake of pirating Stoker's story without paying for the copyright. Stoker's widow sued, and the court ordered that all copies be destroyed – fortunately several escaped and the film was shown in Britain recently.

Of course it creaks today – some sequences are speeded-up and are more like a comic crazy-cop chase than a sinister flight of the vampire; special night-blue tints in the original copies have faded, so it looks as if the night scenes are shot in sunlight – even so, the film is a masterpiece of horror.

'Nosferatu' is another term for vampire, and is mentioned in Stoker's *Dracula*. To avoid copyright, Count Dracula became Graf Orlock. He was portrayed by an actor called Max Schreck, but as 'schreck' is German for 'fright' this may not have been his real name. Whitby became Bremen, and the moment when Orlock rises from his coffin and appears on the deck of a ship is superbly scary, with Schreck's skull-like make-up, tomb-like teeth and long tapering claws.

*Frankenstein* (1931)

The first and finest of the Frankenstein cycle, though *Bride of Frankenstein* four years later has some tremendous (and hilarious) moments which make it worth staying in for when it comes round again on television.

James Whale's direction has compassion as well as horror – though the scene by the lake when the monster (portrayed by Boris Karloff) meets the innocent child and kills her was cut at the time by a number of local censors, who found it too horrific.

Images such as Karloff's plugs in the head and the machine that brings the monster to life have been copied ever since. However, nothing compares to this original, though the recent television version by Christopher Isherwood is splendid on a different level.

*King Kong* (1933)

A collector's item. It has just been re-made at a cost of twelve million pounds with a machine ape that takes five-metre strides, has sixteen different hand movements and can roll its eyes. But can anything compare with or repeat the success of the original? The climax, with the gigantic ape on top of the Empire State Building hurling back the fighter planes that have come to destroy him, is one of the great film moments of all time. The heroine who won

Kong's heart – the last thing she intended – was played by Fay Wray. The hero has the last word: 'Twas Beauty killed the Beast'. The director was Merian C. Cooper.

*The Hunchback of Notre Dame* (1939)
Like *The Phantom of the Opera* and *Dr Jekyll and Mr Hyde*, this was made into several versions. Lon Chaney played in the silents, but it was Charles Laughton who made this part his own in the 1939 version, directed by William Dieterle. It is a lavish production with vast crowd scenes outside the cathedral of Notre Dame, but it is Laughton's performance that makes it a classic. His one-eyed make-up and hunched, shambling walk make his appearance hideous, but you can sense the man underneath. 'I'm deaf, you know,' he tells Esmeralda, '... you would think there couldn't be anything more wrong with me, but I am deaf.'

*Dracula* (1958) released in America as *Horror of Dracula*
The first and best of Hammer Films' revivals on the Dracula theme. Directed by Terence Fisher, it brought Christopher Lee and Peter Cushing together for the first time. Taking their parts seriously (or 'sincerely', as Cushing prefers), they made the impossible convincing. This production brought the Count into the age of colour.

Perhaps you've already seen some of these films, but if you haven't, do watch out for them, as they're sometimes shown on T.V. Of course, you may not agree with the author that these are the best, so why not keep a record of your own favourites?

An ordinary notebook will do, and you should take it with you when you watch a horror film. On a left-hand page, write the name of the film and the date it was made, plus the names of the director and stars if you want. You can always look up details in film books in your library if you don't manage to get them down at the time. When you've seen the film, use the opposite right-hand page to write down the plot and what you thought of it, and put the date at the end. If you see the same film again later, you can add a few more lines. It should be interesting to see whether it seems more or less scary the second (or third) time round!

Decorate your book with cutout pictures and drawings (the spookier the better) on the cover and inside, and you will have a handsome reminder of films you have seen which you might keep and use for years and years!

## Lon Chaney

Possibly the greatest of the horror men was the first – Lon Chaney. He was known as 'The Man of a Thousand Faces' and deserved his title. He was a fine actor in his own right, but such a genius at disguise that the film studios seldom allowed him to appear as himself. Apart from a flair for creating his horrific make-up, he was able to twist his body into extraordinary shapes. There was another reason for his ability to mime in those early silent films – his parents were deaf-mutes, unable to hear him or talk to him, so gesture was all-important.

Chaney's first important role was that of Frog, a fake cripple, in *The Miracle Man* (1920), which made his reputation. His versatility was seen in the following roles: a man without legs in *The Penalty* (1920); *The Hunchback of Notre Dame* (1923); an old lady in white wig and specs in *The Unholy Three* (1925); *Phantom of the Opera* (1925), when he achieved a skull-like effect by pushing a painful object into his nose to widen the nostrils, and discs in his cheeks to project the cheekbones; an 'armless wonder' in *The Unknown* (1927), in which he wore a strait-jacket which was so tight that blood vessels burst in his legs; the insane wax-works manager in *While Paris Sleeps* (1923); a terrifying one-eyed man in *The Road to Mandalay* (1926); a paralysed man in *West of Zanzibar* (1929); and both a Scotland Yard Detective and a horrifying vampire in *London After Midnight* (1927).

Boris Karloff, a struggling young actor at the time, said: 'There was only one Lon Chaney', but he could have said there were a hundred.

Chaney knew that 'the secret of success in Hollywood lies in being different from anyone else. Find something no one else can or will do – and they'll begin to take notice of you! Hollywood is full of competent actors. What the screen needs is individuality!'

His own taste for horror was encouraged by one of his directors, Tod Browning, and together they did their utmost to frighten those early audiences out of the moviehouse, for all these films were silent. Chaney's only 'talkie' was a 1930 re-make of *The Unholy Three*. Playing a crooked ventriloquist, Chaney coped perfectly with the different voices of a dummy, a midget pretending to be a baby, and a sweet old lady with white hair who forgets 'herself' in the witness box and talks in the gruff tones of the man 'she' really is.

Chaney's skill made him the natural choice for his next role – that of the vampire Count Dracula. His studios had bought the film rights, and his old friend and colleague, Tod Browning, was going to direct.

But Chaney was seriously ill. In those days they used dry flakes for snow-scenes, and it is suggested that one of these stuck in his throat and started an infection.

When the shooting of *The Unholy Three* was finished, Chaney suggested that a photograph should be taken of the entire film crew. Then he shook hands with everyone and left. He did not return. Lon Chaney died at the age of forty-four on 26th August, 1930.

## Bela Lugosi

Bela Lugosi replaced Lon Chaney as Count Dracula. A natural choice, for Lugosi had been playing the vampire on the stage in Broadway. He had little need of make-up for he looked sinister already, with strange piercing eyes, and his accent was no problem as he was Hungarian.

Born on 29th October, 1884, his background remains vague. He was either the son of a Baron Lugosi, a banker, or, as some people claim, he took his name from the town where he was born – Lugos – and his first name from the tribe of Bela.

After serving in the Hungarian cavalry he played small film parts in Europe and then came to Hollywood. Though he appeared in a silent version of *Dr Jekyll and Mr Hyde*, he was not successful as an actor until the English stage version of *Dracula* came to New York and he was given the title role. The play ran for two years on Broadway and Lugosi's personal triumph made him the obvious successor to Lon Chaney.

Bela Lugosi had the luck to become the first 'horror star' in the first Hollywood production to be advertised as a 'horror film'. For good measure, the publicity men described it as 'The strangest love a man has ever known'. *Dracula* was an instant success. It is the oldest talkie that still plays commercially and, for all its flaws, it is a masterpiece. The effective opening showing Castle Dracula in the Carpathian Mountains is surprisingly true to Stoker. The sets may be fake, but they haunt the imagination, and even the three vampire women are convincing. Though the attempts at humour are sometimes heavy-handed, there are good moments like the dinner party where Count Dracula says: 'I don't drink', adding *'wine'*, with a sinister smile, as he notices a tempting pin-prick of blood on a guest's hand. But Browning and Lugosi never made the mistake of 'sending up' the story for laughs. They knew that if a vampire is laughed at, he is no longer frightening. *Dracula* was safe in their hands and the public enjoyed being horrified. By 1933, Lugosi was receiving as big a fan-mail as that of any romantic film star, and told the press that 97 per cent of the letters came from women.

It was obvious that the film studios should cash in on the horror cult and think of *Frankenstein* as the follow-up. Bela Lugosi now made the greatest mistake of his life. He was the natural choice for the 'Monster', but was insulted at being offered what he considered an inferior, non-speaking part. He disliked the idea of all that heavy make-up, and wanted his own face to be seen. He turned the part down.

The brilliant British director, James Whale, noticed a young actor having lunch in the studio's canteen. He thought he had possibilities and gave him a film test. He got the part. The actor's name was Boris Karloff, and he became the new 'horror star'.

Lugosi's health began to deteriorate. As early as 1935 he needed medical attention for 'shooting pains in my legs', and in 1955 he asked to be admitted to hospital for treatment. Though he was a wreck, compared to his vitality when he played Count Dracula in 1931, he started work on another film, *The Black Sleep*, when he came out, with the old reliables Lon Chaney Jnr and John Carradine. Lugosi had such difficulty remembering his lines that he was given the part of Casmir, a mute servant. His last role was a scientist in a space film *Plan 9 from Outer Space*. He died on 16th August, 1956, at the age of seventy-two. Lugosi made over a hundred films, but the role of Count Dracula, which earned him £200,000, dominated him right to the end. He was laid to rest in his coffin wearing Dracula's black cloak with its scarlet lining, as he requested, with Dracula's ring on his finger.

## Boris Karloff

Hollywood was lucky – or wise – to choose such fine actors for its horror men. Karloff came to the part of Frankenstein's Monster after several years' experience. As Peter Underwood relates in his excellent biography *Horror Man* (Leslie Frewin 1972), Karloff's real name was William Henry Pratt – no wonder he changed it! He was born in England on 23rd November, 1887, the youngest of eight sons and a daughter living at Camberwell in South London. He never knew his father, who died when he was a baby, and as his mother died a few years later he was brought up by his brothers and a half-sister. His first stage part, appropriately, was the Demon King in a Christmas pantomime at the age of nine. Karloff said he knew then that acting was what he wanted to do for the rest of his life.

In 1909, at the age of twenty-two, he bought a second-class ticket and sailed to Canada to become a farmer. But the 'acting bug' had bitten him, and he joined a theatrical company for a salary of £6 a week, changing his name from Pratt to Karloff. He was on his way, and reached Hollywood in 1917. Over the next fourteen years he had a struggle to make ends meet, but learned his craft, appearing in more than fifty silent films, usually as the villain. The star of his first film was Anna Pavlova, the Russian ballerina, and he also appeared with Douglas Fairbanks Senior, Wallace Beery, John and Lionel Barrymore, and the young Laurence Olivier. All the time he was gaining experience. In 1931 alone he appeared in seventeen films, the climax of which was *Frankenstein*.

'What's the best horror picture you ever made?' Karloff was asked for the rest of his life. The answer was always the same – 'Without a doubt, the original *Frankenstein*.' He added: 'The part was what we call a "natural", any actor who played it was destined for success.' But that was too modest. In spite of his 'horror man' image, Karloff was a kind and gentle man. Lugosi might have portrayed the Monster as something sinister – Karloff made the creature sympathetic. This was his personal triumph.

If Lon Chaney had lived to an old age, he would surely have played Count Dracula *and* the Monster, and become the greatest horror star in history. Karloff now became the new master of disguise. For three weeks, he spent every evening with the film's make-up man, Jack Pierce, and together they created the Monster we think of today – an immense figure with nuts and plugs in its head. Mary Shelley never described the Monster in detail, so they had to start from scratch. Pierce asked himself many questions:

'What would a man look like whose brain had been taken from the head of another man, "transplanted" as it were? How would a hand appear that had been "grafted" on to another arm? How would the eyes of a dead man appear if they were suddenly to open? ... The two metal studs that stuck out of the sides of his neck were inlets for electricity – plugs, not bolts. Don't forget the monster was an electrical gadget and that lightning was his life force ... Also I had read that the Egyptians used to bind some criminals hand and foot and bury them alive. When their blood turned to water after their death, it flowed into their extremities and stretched their arms to gorilla length and swelled their hands and feet and faces to abnormal proportions. I thought this would make a nice touch for the monster, since he was supposed to be made from the corpses of executed felons. So I fixed Karloff up that way. The lizard eyes were made of rubber, as was his false head. I made his arms look longer by shortening the sleeves of his coat. His legs were stiffened by steel struts and two pairs of trousers. His large feet were the boots asphalt-spreaders wear. His finger-nails were blackened with shoe polish...'

The result was tremendous, but it was hell for the actor! When they started filming it took three and a half hours to apply the make-up every morning. Wire clamps pulled down the corners of Karloff's mouth, and the boots weighed eighteen pounds each. At the end of the day, it took another one and a half hours to get it all off and he needed a massage and infra-red treatment to regain the use of his muscles. The metal bolts, or plugs, left two small scars on his neck for some time afterwards. But it was worth all the suffering, and Karloff gave the vital finishing touch by adding his own humanity, which made audiences feel for the Monster who wished to be loved and understood. Karloff had no lines to speak but he talked with his eyes. As the producer, Carl Laemmle, put it: 'Karloff's eyes mirrored the suffering we needed.'

For once, Hollywood even improved on the original, as far as film effects were concerned: the sight of the Monster, the lightning, the brain stolen from a madman – all were new ideas. The result was considered so shocking by the studio that they sneaked the film in a quiet preview in California. When the Monster came in backwards, and then turned round and showed his face, half the audience walked out – and then felt they had to go in again! James Whale, the director, was woken by an angry telephone call in the early morning – 'I can't sleep on account of your picture, so I'm darned if you're going to sleep either.' He realised they had a winner.

*Frankenstein* cost 275,000 dollars to make, but brought in 12 million. In 1938, when the original *Dracula* and *Frankenstein* were shown together on the same bill, they earned more than their first showings. The reason is simple – they were the best.

Fan mail began to flow in for Karloff as it had for Lugosi, but with a difference. Many of the letters came from children who felt sorry for the Monster. 'The children have never fallen for my nonsense,' said Karloff. 'They sit in the cinema with their eyes glued to the screen. They watch the Monster parading his stuff, and now and then give hoots of mock terror or shiver with suppressed excitement, but the moment the word END flashes on the screen, they begin to laugh and chatter away about Karloff and his antics.' The parents found the Monster far more horrifying!

Karloff went on to play other roles, such as *Fu Manchu*, and a gang leader in the famous gangster film *Scarface*. But a follow-up was inevitable and, in 1935, he appeared in *The Bride of Frankenstein*, also directed by James Whale. This is a sequel to the original film. In it, the scientist creates a female mate for the Monster, but when she comes to life she looks at the creature with horror. It is a great moment in a fine film, but Karloff was unhappy that he had to talk this time: 'When the monster did speak I knew that this was eventually going to destroy the character. It did for me anyway.'

He had the sense to realise that he might be forced into inferior versions of *Frankenstein*, just as Lugosi was trapped in the role of *Dracula*. For by now Hollywood's imagination was running out, and a small group of actors were reduced to playing the same parts in the same stories over and over again, though frequently they swapped. After the 'brides' came the sons and daughters:

*Dracula's Daughter* (1936), with Bela Lugosi;
*Son of Frankenstein* (1939) with Lugosi as Igor, a crazy shepherd with a broken neck, and Karloff playing the Monster for the last time;
*Son of Dracula* (1943), with the vampire played by Creighton Chaney, who wanted to be an actor in his own right but was firmly labelled as Lon Chaney Junior by the studios.

There were re-makes of the silents such as *Mark of the Vampire* (1935), a copy of Chaney (Senior's) *London After Midnight*, with Lugosi as the vampire and Lionel Barrymore as the detective. Then all the horror characters were brought together:

*Ghost of Frankenstein* (1942), starring Karloff, with Lon Chaney Jnr playing the Monster;
*Frankenstein Meets the Wolf Man* (1943), with Lugosi as Frankenstein;
*House of Frankenstein* (1944), in which Lugosi plays the Monster, Lon Chaney Jnr the Wolfman, and John Carradine Count Dracula.

But the horror cult was giggling its way out of business. The films became sillier and sillier:

*Abbot and Costello Meet Frankenstein* (1948), with Lugosi and Lon Chaney Jnr;

*Old Mother Riley Meets the Vampire* (1952), an English 'cheapie', teaming Lugosi with Arthur Lucan, a female impersonator;

and *Billy the Kid Versus Dracula* (1966), with poor John Carradine as the Count, looking comic in a top hat.

This was self-inflicted murder as far as horror films were concerned. Never make fun of your vampire. If you do, you lose your audience, and the cinemas were losing them fast. Anyhow, there were enough real horrors in the outside world, with World War Two and its aftermath. It seemed that the public no longer wanted horror films.

Meanwhile, Boris Karloff made his escape. Admittedly he played the stooge part in *Abbot and Costello Meet Dr Jekyll*, and appeared in some dreadful (rather than horrific) films. But he did not sink as low as Lugosi. Instead he returned to the stage on Broadway in *Arsenic and Old Lace*, which was such a success that it ran for four years, and he acted with Danny Kaye in the film *The Secret Life of Walter Mitty*. One of his last films, *Targets* (1969), was the first by the fashionable young director Peter Bogdanovich. He made 160 films altogether and died in February 1969, having returned to England, at the age of eighty-two. When asked for the secret of his energy, he replied: 'Clean living – up to the age of six!'

**Christopher Lee**

By the 1950s it seemed that the horror cult was dead and buried. But, as Jonathan Harker discovered in Castle Dracula, vampires may look dead but they rise again. A year after Lugosi's death the time was ripe for a revival. It took

## Horror on Stage and Screen

place in England with Hammer Films and a little-known actor called Christopher Lee. For millions of young filmgoers, who had never heard the name of Lugosi, Lee became the new Dracula.

Christopher Lee had been acting for ten years, without great success. Tall (1.96 m), with a commanding personality, dark, and strangely foreign, though he was born in London in 1922, Lee did not fit easily into the role of 'leading man'. In spite of his well-cut tweeds, he was too sinister. But he was perfect for the part of the Monster when Hammer decided to remake the great horror films of the 1930s, starting with *The Curse of Frankenstein* – 'I went along and convinced them that I would make a suitable Creature, if only by virtue of my size. I didn't care if they made me totally unrecognisable; I wasn't getting anywhere looking like myself, so I though that perhaps people would take a little more notice of me if I looked like nothing on earth. The result was the biggest grossing film in the history of the British cinema in relation to cost.'

It was obvious that Hammer Films should follow this success with *Dracula* in 1958, released in America as *Horror of Dracula*. Hammer's horror was something new – in glorious, glossy colour. When blood flowed, you could see it was red! Lee was lucky in having such a fine actor as Peter Cushing as his co-star. Cushing played the role of Mr Right (such as the vampire hunter Van Helsing) against Lee's Mr Wrong, and lent his personal sincerity to the part. Both men played it straight, which added to the impact.

One detail that should not be overlooked was Christopher Lee's *fangs!* Lugosi had never bared his fangs, but Lee plunged his with relish into the white necks of beautiful girls. Then there were such superb effects as the crumbling of Dracula into dust at the end of the film after Van Helsing has jumped on to the table, making the sign of the crucifix with the giant candlesticks, before pulling down the heavy curtains to let in the light of day.

The cult of Dracula started again. Christopher Lee went on to play him in six more films for Hammer, and became a world star. This is how he explained Dracula's appeal to audiences, when the author visited him at his home in London's Cadogan Square:

> 'He has a strange dark heroism. He offers the illusion of immortality, the subconscious wish we all have for limitless power ... a man of tremendous brain and physical strength ... he is either a reincarnation or he has never died. In many ways, he is everything people would like to be – the anti-hero, the heroic villain.'

He spoke as if he had met him!

But Lee began to be trapped in the part, just like Lugosi. As an admirer of Bram Stoker's original novel, he looks back on that first production with particular pleasure:

> 'That was the first time I had played Dracula and in that film he did resemble Bram Stoker's creation in many ways, except in appearance, which was wrong and has remained wrong in every subsequent film version of the story. The Dracula of the book wore a coat, while all this business of cloaks and opera capes comes from the old Universal pictures. The idea of a man living in the depths of Transylvania, dressed up in white tie and tails and a cape is really quite ridiculous.'

## Horror on Stage and Screen

So it is easy to understand Lee's indignation as Count Dracula moved even further from Transylvania and was cast in such unlikely settings as Chelsea, in swinging London, in *Dracula A. D. 1972*.

It cannot have been easy, but Christopher Lee at last managed to break free from Count Dracula, with whom he had become identified. He even resigned from the Presidency of the Dracula Society, explaining: 'I am no longer associated with the screen portrayal of the character.' He has proved his versatility as an actor with his success as Mycroft Holmes, Sherlock's brother, and more recently as a James Bond villain. And he has played other parts for Hammer, such as Rasputin, the Mummy, and Chung King in *The Terror of the Tongs*, where he had little to do except look evil and Chinese! Bot, like it or not (and he does not), for millions of people Christopher Lee *is* Dracula.

One day Lee may well return as the Count, but only if the film is true to Bram Stoker's novel, which he admires so much. Alternatively, if a film is made about Stoker's life, which has been suggested, Lee could play Count Dracula and the great Shakespearian actor, Sir Henry Irving, and Vincent Price could play Stoker.

### The future of the horror film

In recent years it has seemed as though horror films might once again laugh themselves out of business. Count Dracula has been seen in London's trendy King's Road, David Niven played a comic Dracula in *Vampira* (1973), Hammer Films launched 'The first Kung Fu Horror Spectacular' with *The Legend of the Golden Vampires*, and Mel Brooks made *Young Frankenstein*.

But by now the cult of Dracula has reached such international proportions that he cannot be allowed to die. His world-wide appeal is extraordinary, when you stop to think of it – to date more than a hundred films have been made on the Dracula/Vampire theme.

Vampire films have been produced in Spain, Italy, Germany, Mexico, Canada, the Philippines, Turkey and South Korea, but at the moment Spain is making the greatest number, and an actor called Paul Naschy is the star. In America, his name is not even mentioned on the posters for the dubbed versions of his films, which are lurid. 'New SICKENING HORROR to make your Stomach Turn and Flesh Crawl ... See the Wolf Monster attack – Lusting, Slashing, Ripping' is the recommendation for *Frankenstein's Bloody Terror*. *Dracula Versus Frankenstein* is described simply as 'The Ultimate in Horror'.

Meanwhile, America has revived the Dracula cult herself, with intriguing variations such as a black Dracula in *Blacula* (1972), and *Count Yorga' Vampire* (1970), which is set in present-day Los Angeles. Returning to the original, BBC Television have filmed a 2½-hour *Dracula* true to Stoker's novel. With the French actor Louis Jourdan as Count Dracula, this was produced as a gory Christmas treat for 1977.

With Andy Warhol's recent *Dracula*, the appeal of Bram Stoker's character seems, incredibly, to be as strong as ever. No literary creation has proved so fascinating, both to distinguished film directors and to audiences all over the world. We have plenty of frights to look forward to!

# 6
# ALMOST HUMAN

*'The creatures I had seen were not men,
had never been men. They were animals –
humanised animals – triumphs of vivisection.'*

(The Island of Dr Moreau
by H. G. Wells)

## The Elephant Man

He was not really horrible at all – that was his tragedy. Neither was he an animal, but he was called the Elephant Man because 'he was an object of horror to those who saw him'.

His real name was John Merrick and he suffered from a terrible disease, described by Sir Frederick Treves, Surgeon Extraordinary to Queen Victoria, as 'neurofibromatosis'. This caused hideous swellings under his skin and it could not be treated. He could hardly speak and could only walk with the help of a stick.

In many ways, he was a caricature of poor Quasimodo, *The Hunchback of Notre Dame*. And, like Quasimodo, who worshipped his Esmeralda with all the sensitivity of a Romeo, the ugliness of the Elephant Man concealed an ordinary human being. No, that is wrong: in his innocence he was better than ordinary.

Frederick Treves first saw him in the East End of London, where he was being exhibited in a grocer's shop. Outside was a life-size portrait of 'a frightful creature that could only have been possible in a nightmare. It was the figure of a man with the characteristics of an elephant.' But Treves thought 'there was more of the man than of the beast. This fact, that it was still human, was the most repellent attribute of the creature.' He said there was nothing pathetic, as of someone deformed, nor grotesque, but 'merely the loathing insinuation of a man being changed into an animal.' To make the picture more horrific, a jungle scene was painted in the background. Admission was 2d.

The door of the shop was locked but Treves found the owner in a pub nearby, and the man agreed to a private view for the price of a shilling. He pulled the curtains back to reveal a figure crouching on a stool, covered by a blanket. The creature never moved. Treves found it 'the embodiment of loneliness', and described what he saw in these words:

> 'Outside the sun was shining. The showman ordered the creature to stand and the blanket fell to the ground. There stood revealed the most disgusting specimen of humanity that I have ever seen. In the course of my profession I had come upon lamentable deformities of the face due to injury or disease as well as mutilations ... but at no time had I met with such a degraded version of a human being as this lone figure displayed.
>
> 'He was naked to the waist, his feet were bare, he wore a pair of threadbare trousers that had once belonged to some fat gentleman's dress suit.
>
> 'From the painting in the street I had imagined the Elephant Man to be of gigantic size. This, however, was a little man below the average height and made to look shorter by the bowing of his back.'

The creature's most striking feature was his enormous head, with a bony growth on the forehead that almost hid one of his eyes. Another growth on his upper jaw turned the lip inside out. In the painting this had been made to look like a tusk. Treves remarked that 'The face was no more capable of expression than a block of gnarled wood.'

Ironically, the most horrific touch of all was that though one arm was shapeless, the other was as perfect and delicate as a woman's. Merrick was twenty-one years old.

Treves managed to smuggle the Elephant Man, disguised in a vast hat and cloak, to the Medical College where he lectured on anatomy. He made a physical examination and returned the creature to the shop. But the next day, when he came back to find out more about the Elephant Man, he found the shop empty. The show had been closed by the police.

Treves believed, and hoped, that Merrick had been an imbecile from birth. He would be unable to understand the full horror of his life – exhibited as a monster, stared at with disgust by the people who paid to see him, and only glimpsing the outside world from a peep-show in the showman's cart.

The police acted out of kindness in closing the shows, but it meant that Merrick was shunted from town to town, never finding peace. Two years passed, and the exasperated showman took his exhibition to Belgium but it was banned there too, considered 'too brutal'. This was the worst thing that could have happened to the Elephant Man, for now he was no longer of any use, and became an object to be disposed of. The showman did this with terrible cruelty, putting Merrick on a train to London after stealing his savings.

As Treves remarked, what was Merrick to do? 'He knew no more of London than he knew of Peking. All he wanted was to hide.' At Liverpool Street Station the police rescued him from the crowds and put him in the safety of a third class waiting room. They were baffled, for his mutterings might have been Arabian, and then they found the card that Treves had given him two years earlier when he examined him in the East End.

Miraculously, or with an intelligence that no one had suspected, Merrick had clung to his card all this time and now it saved him. 'He seemed pleased to see me,' wrote Treves of their meeting, when he was summoned to the station, 'but he was nearly done. The journey and want of

## Almost Human

food had reduced him to the last stage of exhaustion.'

Treves took him to his hospital and placed him in a separate room used for emergency cases. This was against the rules, but the Chairman agreed that Merrick could not be cast out again. He wrote to *The Times*, explaining the case of the Elephant Man and asking for money to help him. With remarkable generosity, the public sent enough money in one week to look after Merrick for life. A small apartment was found at the back of the hospital, opening onto a courtyard. A bathroom was added, for Merrick needed a bath at least once a day as he smelt so bad.

Merrick now had a home and found himself among friends for the first time in his life.

The change was remarkable. Treves began to understand his mutterings and talked to him constantly, for Merrick was thirsty for knowledge. He began to read books, especially love stories, which he believed were true. He could not remember his past, or did not wish to, but believed his mother had been beautiful and loving. Yet it was obvious that he had been abandoned as a baby.

Though he had lived without hope as a 'strange beast in a cage', part of the fun of the fair, he was now an affectionate person with no bitterness. But he was unable to believe his good luck, and expected to be moved yet again. He asked Treves, pathetically, 'When I am next moved can I go to a blind asylum or to a lighthouse?' In such places, where people could not see him, his ugliness would not matter.

He became less frightened. He began to trust the nurses who looked after him, but Treves realised what a difference it would make if a woman came to see him because she wanted to and not from duty, and so he arranged such a meeting:

'I asked a friend of mine, a young and pretty widow, if she thought she could enter Merrick's room with a smile, wish him good morning and shake him by the hand. She said she could, and she did. The effect upon poor Merrick was not quite what I had expected. As he let go her hand he bent his head on his knees and sobbed until I thought he would never cease. The interview was over. He told me afterwards that this was the first woman who had ever smiled at him. From this day the transformation of Merrick commenced and he began to change, little by little, from a hunted thing into a man. It was a wonderful change to witness and one that never ceased to fascinate me.'

Many friendly visits followed. People brought ornaments to decorate his room, and one day the Princess of Wales, later Queen Alexandra, sat by his chair and talked to him as if he were a friend. Later she sent him Christmas cards and a signed photograph which became his most treasured possession. 'I am happy every hour of the day,' he told the man who had saved him, but Treves noted that he was unable to smile: 'Whatever his delight might be, his face remained expressionless. He could weep but he could not smile.' His one sadness was a yearning for romance. It was the old, universal story of Beauty and the Beast, and when he spoke of living among the blind, Treves felt that Merrick had the faint hope of winning the love of a woman who could not see him.

One ambition was achieved – a visit to the theatre. Careful plans were laid, with the help of Mrs Kendal the actress, and Merrick was brought in a closed carriage to Drury Lane, through the Royal Entrance, and up to a box. He arrived unnoticed because three nurses sat in front to screen him, wearing full evening dress. The expedition was a total success:

> 'One has often witnessed the unconstrained delight of a child at his first pantomime, but Merrick's rapture was more intense. . . . Here was a being with the brain of a man, the fancies of a youth and the imagination of a child. He was awed. Merrick talked of the pantomime for weeks and weeks. To him, as to a child with the gift of make-believe, everything was real: the palace was the home of kings, the princess was of royal blood, the fairies were as undoubted as the children in the street.'

He did not like the giants, and was mystified by the clowns.

Another great treat was Merrick's first holiday in the country. He sent delighted letters to Treves, describing a fierce dog he made friends with and enclosing some wild flowers which were quite ordinary but seemed rare and precious to him.

Six months later, Merrick was found dead in his bed. His head was so heavy that he could not sleep lying down as most people do, but had to sit up with his back supported by pillows while his head rested on his knees. Treves thought that on that final night Merrick had tried to sleep 'like other people', and had dislocated his neck. 'Thus it came about that his death was due to the desire that dominated his life – the pathetic but hopeless desire to be like other people.'

But his life had ended happily. Treves gave him this tribute:

> 'As a specimen of humanity, Merrick was ignoble and repulsive, but the spirit of Merrick, if it could be seen in the form of the living, would assume the figure of an upstanding and heroic man, smooth browed and clean of limb, and with eyes that flashed undaunted courage.'

A noble epitaph from the excellent man who befriended him.

## Wolf children

In 1850, in Central Europe, a baby was discovered in a forest by a pack of wolves. His parents had died and they looked after him, teaching him their skills. He grew up more wolf than boy, eating raw meat and unable to speak except for snarls and grunts. One day, when he was hunting, he was shot by the owner of a travelling circus and captured. The circus badly needed an attraction and 'Etoile', as he became known, was exhibited as the wolf-boy....

This is not true. It is the opening of the film *Legend of the Werewolf*, made in Britain in 1975. But it could have been true. One explanation for the legend of the werewolf is that people might have seen such a boy running with a wolf pack (see Chapter 3).

The wolf is persecuted unfairly. When a Canadian newspaper offered a hundred dollars to anyone who could prove that a wolf had made an unprovoked attack, no one was able to collect it. A wolf hunt was organised in 1972 in Quebec with a prize for the hunter who killed the most – the idea was to wipe out entire packs. This was called off because of hostile public reaction, and rightly so. There is evidence that the standards of the wolf are at least as high as our own. The female vixen mates with one wolf and

## Almost Human

remains faithful for life, and when adult wolves are killed, another pair will look after the cubs.

If a child is abandoned or lost, a vixen may mother it and bring it up. This is what happened to Romulus and Remus, the legendary founders of Rome, who were taken from their real mother and suckled by a she-wolf. It is the subject of Kipling's *Jungle Book*, in which a wood-cutter's child called Mowgli crawls away from home and is rescued from a tiger by a family of wolves. Mowgli grows up learning the laws of the jungle, but finally returns to his human family. He promises to return one day, and the mother wolf pleads with him: 'Come soon . . . little naked son of mine; for listen, child of man, I loved thee more than ever I loved my cubs.'

This is fiction, but such stories are based on fact. The French film *L'Enfant Sauvage* (The Wild Boy), made by François Truffaut in 1970, is based on the true incident of the Wild Boy of Aveyron. Early in the nineteenth century the boy was found in the woods, living on nuts and berries like an animal. At first he was declared an incurable idiot, until a French doctor (played by Truffaut in the film) took him under his personal care. The boy learnt to stand up, speak a little, and do simple tasks – but that was all. He never became a normal human being, because he had lived like an animal for too long.

The story of the Wolf Children of Midnapore is the most interesting and best documented of all such cases. It happened in India, in this century. The inhabitants of a village in Bengal were so frightened by a 'man ghost' they had seen on their outskirts that they asked for the help of the Reverend J. A. L. Singh, missionary to the local orphanage. They hoped he might be able to perform an exorcism.

After building a tree platform in the jungle, near the

place where the 'man ghost' had been seen, the Reverend Singh and his companions climbed on top and waited patiently for an hour. He recorded the event that followed in his diary:

> 'October 9, 1920: All of a sudden, a grown wolf came out from one of the holes, which was very smooth on account of their constant egress and ingress. This animal was followed by another of the same size and kind. The second was followed by a third, closely followed by two cubs one after the other. The holes did not permit two together.
>
> 'Close after the cubs came the 'ghost' – a hideous looking being – hands, feet and body like a human being; but the head was a big ball of some thing covering the shoulders and the upper portions of the bust, leaving only a sharp contour of the face visible, and it was human. Close at its heels there came another awful creature like the first, but smaller in size. Their eyes were bright and piercing, unlike human eyes.
>
> 'The first ghost appeared on the ground up to its bust, and placing its elbows on the edge of the hole looked at this side and that side, and jumped out. It looked all round the place from the mouth of the hole before it leaped out to follow the cubs. It was followed by another tiny ghost of the same kind, behaving in the same manner. Both of them ran on all fours.
>
> 'My friends at once levelled their guns to shoot at the ghosts. They would have killed them if they had not been dissauded by me. I held their barrels and presented the field glasses ... and told them I was sure that these ghosts were human children.'

## Almost Human

After a closer look, they agreed, except for a terrified villager called Chunarem. The Reverend Singh asked Chunarem to help him dig the children up, but the villager refused flatly, in spite of the money, 'You are all here only for a day,' he said, 'but we have to live here. When you go away these Manush Baghas (men ghosts) will play havoc with us and would kill us all.'

So the missionary had to go to another village where the men knew nothing of the ghosts. He hired workers and they started to dig the wolves' lair a week later, with instructions not to shoot. While they were at work one wolf appeared and raced into the jungle, then the second, equally frightened, but the third, the mother wolf, flew at the men in rage, howling, gnashing her teeth and fiercely defending the hole and her young inside it.

Singh watched with admiration. He was amazed at the strength of the mother's feelings for creatures which she had probably originally brought in as food for her cubs.

Meanwhile, the others pierced the wolf with arrows and she fell dead. Then the door was dug out and they entered the cave. The two cubs and the two 'ghosts' were huddled together snarling in one corner.

Sending for several big sheets, the men succeeded in separating them. The cubs were given to the villagers and the other two – the ghosts – were brought to the house of the frightened villager, Chunarem. This was asking for trouble and, sure enough, Chunarem and his wife fled in horror. Curiously, the missionary did not return for several days. When he did, he found that the children had been left without food or water and were in a terrible state. He sprinkled cold water on their faces and gave them some to drink, and then carried them home.

For the head of an orphanage, Singh was surprisingly stupid. He had forced the children into another terrible transition. They had changed course already, from the weaning by human milk to wolf milk; they ran swiftly on all fours to keep pace with the cubs; their eyes had grown used to the dark; their sense of smell was highly developed. Remarkable though this was, they had no choice. They had to behave like wolves or die. Now they did not know what to do or, indeed, what they were.

Feeding was a problem which he solved at first by tearing up his handkerchief and rolling it into a wick. He dipped one end into a cupful of tea and the other into the child's mouth, and in this way got them to drink. But the change back to human life was not easy. The children's health grew worse and their bodies became covered with deep sores. Then they seemed to recover and grew stronger on a diet of raw milk and raw meat.

Singh, who does not seem to have been imaginative, named the girls Kamala and Amala. He guessed one was aged eight and the other eighteen months. He does not seem to have known, however, if they had been abandoned or stolen by the wolf from the cornfields.

Soon they were crawling, not upright but not entirely on all fours as before. In their lair it would have been difficult to stand up even if they had wanted to, but now they had freedom of movement. They were accepted by the other children in the orphanage as neglected children who were particularly weak. They took a liking to a year-old baby who was just starting to walk, but one day, discovering that he was different, they turned on him savagely and he never went near them again. All the time they made no sound, apart from howling at night.

## Almost Human

The missionary was fascinated by the ease with which the children's limbs had become like those of animals, to make their movements easier, when they only had the wolves to copy. To do him justice he tried to avoid the sensational publicity that began to focus on Midnapore as the story of the children spread by word of mouth. Mrs Singh was a kindly, calm woman who spent hours massaging the children's limbs, as they learnt new movements. From lapping their food like dogs, they took it by hand. Their eyes grew accustomed to the light, so that day and night became separate. The mother wolf had not been able to give them a sense of humour, but she had not taught them anything evil. They knew no malice, no cowardice, no jealousy. Though she was unable to laugh, Kamala cried when her companion Amala died on 21st September, 1921 – two tears fell from her eyes.

Kamala stood upright for the first time two years later, though she continued to run on all fours. Her natural distrust of humans gradually disappeared. She wore clothes, she no longer ate raw meat, and by 1927 she could make herself understood. By then only the bumps on her knees and elbows, her flared nostrils and her bent shape made her different from the other children at the orphanage, who were extremely fond of her. Even so, her intelligence was like that of a three-year-old, and her speech was limited to thirty words when she was sixteen. She died on 4th November, 1929. The doctor's certificate stated that 'Kamala, commonly known as the Wolf Girl, a girl of the Reverend Singh's Orphanage, expired this morning at 4 a.m.'

It is also possible to conclude from this strange story that human children can adapt to animal life with surprising ease. This seems the most logical explanation for the mythical werewolf.

## The leopard men

They sound colourful, but the things they did were horrible. It helps to understand them if you remember that Africa has witnessed some of the first and fiercest clashes between man and animal. It is not surprising that primeval instincts have lingered on for centuries in regions which have remained primitive for so long. Hunter and hunted – the two were inseparable, almost interchangeable. The Bushmen of South Africa used to give their children the hearts of leopards to eat, to make them brave. If the heart could achieve this, imagine the power of the soul. One hundred years ago it was commonly believed in West Africa that if a witch doctor and a dangerous animal such as a leopard became blood brothers, the witch doctor would gain power and the animal would become his 'familiar' or slave and kill his enemies for him. This special relationship would last until the death of either party.

Such beliefs were widespread along the coasts of French Guinea and Sierra Leone, down to Dahomey, Nigeria, and the Congo basin. Leopard Societies flourished in these regions, not always in secrecy. In 1895, a *Human Leopard Society Ordinance* was passed in Sierra Leone, punishing anyone who possessed a leopard skin or the three-pronging weapon that imitated a leopard's claws. During the next seven years a court sentenced eighty-seven men to death for leopard murders. These men believed they shared the strength of a leopard once they wore his skin, in the same way as the *berserkirs* of the North, who wore bearskins when they raided villages.

In 1939, the American writer Negley Farson (the author's father) made a journey across Africa, which he recorded in his book *Behind God's Back*. He found evidence of the leopard men in the twentieth century and wrote:

## Almost Human

'You will find today the most savage, hideous human beings left in Africa. And it is a fact that the Society of the Leopard still carries on, is even thought to be growing, in these parts; of men with steel claws who kill women and eat parts of them. . . . This Society of the Leopards is so secret, so powerful, that even the native police are too terrified to inform on them. They are, as the Governor said, an almost insoluble African mystery . . . the African *lives all his life in a constant state of dread*. He's afraid of the witch doctor, he lives in terror of the evil spirits, he is afraid of the dark, the things that are in it, he lives in continual horror of offending the leopard men.'

The leopard men took advantage of this 'horror' in the Mau Mau troubles, which resulted in the arrest of Jomo Kenyatta in 1952, though he became President later. One of the 'terrorists' was Dedan Kimathi, who wore a leopard skin and leopard hood for his attacks until he was captured.

Undoubtedly, part of the power of the Leopard Men came from the belief that when they dressed as leopards they *were* leopards, possessing the strength of the animal and inspired by his spirit.

### The vampire bat

This is not a mythical or fictional beast but a real mammal. It lives mainly in Central and South America, parts of the West Indies and Java. The bat makes a small bite, like the nick of a razor blade, and licks its victim's blood. Humans are seldom attacked, and the most common victims are horses and cattle. The bat breaks the skin of the neck so gently that they are hardly aware of it, yet they weaken and die from loss of blood. This is not the greatest danger, however, for bats are notorious carriers of rabies and spread the infection.

Bats are night animals, with tiny, fierce eyes and large ears to help their hearing when they fly in the dark. In order to avoid obstacles they make shrill squeaking noises as they fly and listen to echoes bouncing off things.

In view of their gentle attacks in the dead of night, the sharp little pin-pricks left by their bites and their odd appearance, with gnarled little faces and cloak-like wings, it is not wholly surprising that people should relate vampire bats to human vampires. Count Dracula is able to appear in the shape of a bat, and Van Helsing describes them dramatically:

> 'Can you tell me why in the Pampas, ay and elsewhere, there are bats that come at night and open the veins of cattle and horses and suck dry their veins; how in some islands of the Western seas there are bats which hang on trees all day, and that when sailors sleep on deck, because that it is hot, flit down on them, and then – and then in the morning are found dead men, white as even Miss Lucy was?'

Of course Lucy was not bitten by a bat, but by Count Dracula. But it is true that vampires bats do need to drink large amounts of blood every day to keep alive. There is something in their saliva which prevents blood clots, so that blood can run slowly from their incision for several hours.

An attack by a vampire bat was reported in the *Daily Telegraph* newspaper on 28th April, 1976. Major John Blashford-Snell, a thirty-three-year-old explorer in the jungles of Panama, was asleep in his tent when a bat flew down and sank its teeth in his left foot. He says he did not feel the bite, but: 'I awoke as it flew off to find the bedclothes covered with blood. I saw the bat, which had an eight-inch wing-span, disappear out of the tent. They bite so gently that you don't feel it until it is too late.'

Judging by the quantity of blood on the bed, the Major reckoned the bat must have had about half a pint. He was driven straight to the city of Panama for a series of anti-rabies injections, as it could have proved fatal.

## The Black Dog of Death

It was the 'familiar' of witches, but was hardly a pet. The dog is usually described by people who see it as being jet black, shoulder high, with human eyes and an almost human intelligence glaring from them as it bares its teeth and snarls.

D. A. Mac-Manus was an expert on Irish superstition, and was once told by an old man that no one dared to cross the bridge at Pontoon after midnight because it was guarded by a great black dog. Mac-Manus checked up and found that many people believed this story, including one man who had stopped by the bridge to pump up his bicycle tyre. Looking up, he saw a large black dog jump over the wall and stare at him. He muttered a prayer and rode off as quickly (and bumpily) as he could, with his tyre still flat. The curious thing is that no one thought this was a real dog. On the contrary, they pointed out that there were so many black labradors in the Irish countryside at the time that they could have told the difference instantly. Like the wail of the Irish banshee, a glimpse of the animal was taken as a warning of death.

In farming communities in Central Europe, the black dog was once respected as a harvest spirit. When the wind set the corn moving, like waves on the sea, the peasants would say 'The mad Dog is in the corn'. To stop their children trampling over the cornfields when they collected flowers, they warned them 'the big dog sits in the corn' or 'the wolf will tear you to pieces'. The peasant who cut the last sheaf was called the Wheat-Dog or Rye-Wolf, and in some regions had to play the part by pretending to bite the other harvesters, howling like a wolf. In parts of Germany the last sheaf was made into the shape of a giant dog or wolf, with legs of stalks and a tail of wheat-ears. Then it was carried in a harvest procession to the farm, where it was sprinkled with brandy and set to rest on a high shelf in the parlour. Occasionally it was made in a human form and dressed in clothes, like a scarecrow, and this shows that the harvest-spirit was thought of as being half-human, half-animal. If a harvester was slack, or something went wrong, it was said that 'the White Dog has passed near him' – white being weak compared to the strength of black.

Such superstitions were part of a murder outside the small village of Lower Quinton near Stratford-on-Avon which took place on Saint Valentine's Day, 1945. A seventy-four-year-old farmer, Charles Walton, was found beneath a willow tree, pinned to the ground with his hay-fork and slashed to death with his razor-sharp bill-hook which he used for trimming hedges. The police were mystified by the brutality of the killing and the lack of motive. But rumours began to spread and it was reported in the press as 'a weird ritual killing' ... 'a legend come to life ... in a haunted corner of England where the powers of witchcraft live on.' One headline referred to The Black Dog of Death, for the village had a legend that a strange animal, 'larger than most dogs and with unearthly, burning eyes, appeared from nowhere and disappeared into nowhere'

12 'Upon its head, with red extended mouth and solitary eye of fire, sat the hideous beast whose craft had seduced me into murder . . . I had walled up the monster within the tomb!' A horrific moment from Edgar Allan Poe's story *The Black Cat*.

13 (*above*) The man who dreamt up Dracula – Bram Stoker.

14 (*below*) Christopher Lee as Count Dracula meets his match.

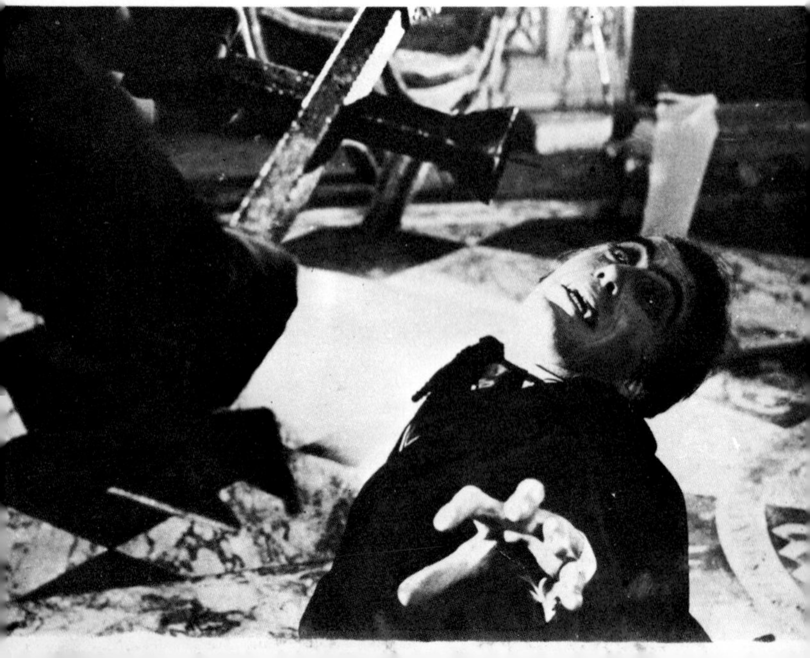

15 (*above*) The first Dracula film, *Nosferatu,* was made in 1922.

16 (*below*) Bela Lugosi as the Count in his most famous role – *Dracula* (1931).

17 (*above*) An old engraving of Glamis Castle in Scotland. Legend tells of a secret room in which a monster, the Horror of Glamis, is hidden. The whereabouts of the room is known only to the Earls of Strathmore, owners of the Castle.

18 (*opposite above*) Highgate Cemetery in north London was designed by the foremost architects and landscape gardeners of the Victorian age. In 1970 it was invaded by 'vampire hunters', who broke into graves and overturned tombstones.

19 (*opposite, below*) Borley Rectory in Suffolk has often been called 'the most haunted house in England'. Sightings of a ghostly nun have been reported even after the complete destruction of the house by fire in 1939.

20 Prince Vlad V of Wallachia, also known as Vlad the Impaler, lived in the fifteenth century. He was an extremely cruel man who especially enjoyed impaling his enemies on spikes, so that they would suffer a long and agonising death. This woodcut shows him tucking into his lunch under a row of writhing bodies.

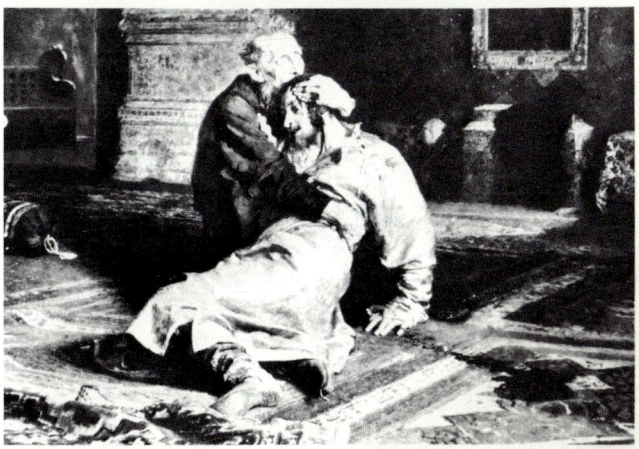

21 (*top*) Rasputin the 'mad monk' lived in the court of Tsar Nicholas of Russia. His amazing powers of healing led to his murder by enemies jealous of his influence.

22 (*below*) Ivan the Terrible of Russia murders his son.

23 During six weeks in 1888 five women were knifed to death within a few square kilometres of London streets. The murderer wrote letters to the papers signing himself 'Jack the Ripper', and caused panic throughout England. His killings became increasingly gruesome and then stopped as suddenly as they had begun. The Ripper's identity was never discovered, and even today new theories are still being put forward. You can read the story of Jack the Ripper in Chapter 8. This old print shows a vigilante patrol watching a suspicious character passing along the dimly lit streets of London's East End.

when someone was about to die, and such a creature had been spotted just before the murder.

In 1885 a Warwickshire parson had recorded the story of a ploughboy who saw such a dog on nine evenings at dusk. Farmworkers laughed at his vivid description, but on the ninth day the dog turned into a headless woman gliding past the boy with her silk dress rustling. The next morning the boy's sister was dead. And the name of the ploughboy was Charles Walton – the same as that of the murdered man in Lower Quinton. Villagers seized on the possible connection. The impalement by the pitchfork was compared to the stake thrust through the heart of a vampire, and it was noticed that the wound on the dead man's chest was in the shape of a cross.

In spite of all their experience, detectives were said to have been horrified by the look of terror on the dead man's face. They learnt of a similar murder in 1875, in a village nearby, when a woman was pinned to the ground and slashed in the form of a cross. The murderer claimed that he did this because the woman was a witch. Inevitably, the murder at Lower Quinton became known as The Witchcraft Murder.

The American expert on witchcraft, Margaret Mead, went to the village in 1950 and concluded she was *almost* satisfied that the murder was a witchcraft killing. But almost is not good enough, and though the police Inspector investigating the case returned there on Saint Valentine's Eve for the next few years, no further proof was found.

Now that the case is no longer sensational, the facts seem straightforward. The cross-shaped wound would be caused by a natural slashing movement, and as for the look of terror on the dead man's face, it would be surprising if the victim had smiled at his murderer! After all, the man had just pinned him to the ground and was about to kill him with a bill-hook. The police now have a more sensible theory – that the murder was one of local revenge. And the Black Dog of Death? We must not forget him, but the explanation is disappointing. There was a perfectly ordinary black dog roaming the district at the time. No doubt, if he startled people at night, he must have looked a bit alarming!

A case involving a black *headless* dog was reported as recently as 1976. On 28th June, the *Daily Telegraph* newspaper reported an interview with a retired builder in his seventies, Joe Hatherill, who lives in a village opposite the home of Princess Anne and Captain Mark Phillips, Gatcombe Park in the Cotswolds. He claimed he had seen a headless dog on four different occasions:

> 'It is a big black dog without a head which brushes up against you. I have lived here for fifty-five years and I promise you I am not lying. Lots of my friends have seen it.... I had a friend called Fred Webb, a farmer who is now sadly dead. One night he came down this road driving a friend in his pony and trap when this dog appeared. It frightened the life out of him and he never came along this road again. He was a big man too, six foot tall and sixteen or seventeen stone...'

## The Nuckelavee

Among the mythical beasts are many entertaining creatures, like the Mermaid – half-fish, half-woman; the Minotaur – half-bull, half-man; even the good-living, wine-loving Satyr, who is half-goat. Some are bad, like the fiery Dragon and the Kraken, a sea-serpent who wrecked sailing ships and brought them to the bottom of the ocean, but by far the nastiest is the Nuckelavee, described by Katherine

M. Briggs in her book *The Personnel of Fairyland*. It may not sound all that bad – a Scottish imp that lived in the sea – but it looked horrible.

When a Nuckelavee came ashore he rode a horse, and many people thought rider and horse were one creature, for the horse was hideous too. The Nuckelavee's head was ten times larger than an ordinary man's and his mouth resembled a pig's. Worst of all, he had no hair on his body, for he had no skin! His raw flesh showed its twisting yellow veins and black blood. An eye-witness referred to a huge man with no legs, arms that swung to the ground and a head that rolled backwards and forwards – not a pretty sight!

Not surprisingly, the Nuckelavee had bad breath too! It was so strong that it destroyed plants and made animals ill. Consequently, he was blamed for any failure of crops or sickness of cattle. This probably explains the legend – he was simply a 'scapegoat'.

## The Lambton Worm

This mythical creature was reported in the Middle Ages. Its story is interesting because of the comparison with Bram Stoker's 'White Worm', which you can read about later in this chapter. It was discovered in the Wear River in the north of England by John Lambton, near his ancestral home. He had gone fishing on a Sunday, but caught this creature instead. It had nine holes on each side of its mouth, and he thought he had landed the Devil! After bringing it on land, he threw it into a deep well and was glad to be rid of it – or so he thought. However, several weeks later the Worm squirmed out again and started to raid the countryside, attacking cows, gulping down lambs and frightening everyone.

Lambton, who felt responsible, joined the Crusades as a penance, and spent the next seven years out of the country. When he returned, his father told him that the Worm had grown more savage, uprooting trees and killing people. It came to Lambton Hall every day demanding milk, and the people were too scared to refuse. John Lambton tried to kill the Worm, but with no success. When he sliced it into pieces, they joined together again. At last he went to the Wise Woman of Brageford, who told him the secret way of killing the Worm, but warned him that he had to kill the first living thing he met afterwards, otherwise the Lambton family would be cursed for nine generations.

Lambton put on a special suit of armour, and after an hour's battle, in which the Worm tried to squeeze him to death, he killed it. Overjoyed, he blew a blast on his bugle as he returned to Lambton Hall as a signal to release Boris, his unfortunate hound, who would run to greet him and be killed as 'the first living thing'. But his plans went wrong. In his excitement his old father hurried to meet him, and Lambton could not bear to kill him.

Sure enough, the next nine generations of the Lambton men were pursued by trouble. As the Wise Woman predicted, none of them died in their beds, but at least the terror of the Lambton Worm was over.

## The Island of Dr Moreau

H. G. Wells was a brilliant writer with a vivid imagination, shown in such books as *The Invisible Man* and *The War of the Worlds*. In *The Island of Dr Moreau* he touches on a universal theme – the attempt to make a man live longer by injecting him with parts of animals. But Wells's fictional Dr Moreau did it the other way round – he tried to change animals into men, with hideous results.

## Almost Human

The story, set in 1887, is told as though it were true. A shipwrecked man is picked up by a passing vessel, bound for Hawaii. Two passengers are to be dropped off on a remote island, and the narrator notices that one man looks peculiar – he is misshapen, short, broad and clumsy, with a crooked back, a hairy neck and a head sunk between his shoulders. The dogs on board howl whenever he comes near them.

Montgomery, the other man, persuades the narrator to leave the ship with them. Arriving at the island, he finds it inhabited by 'Beast Men'. He believes they have once been animals, but now they are even able to talk. These creatures are the results of Dr Moreau's experiments, and the horror of the book lies in the agony the animals have to suffer.

Asked why he has chosen the human form as his model, the doctor replies: 'I suppose there is something in the human form that appeals to the artistic turn of mind more powerfully than any animal shape can.'

When he is accused of cruelty, he defends himself by claiming that 'The study of Nature makes a man at last as remorseless as Nature.' He has created monsters almost for the fun of it and has also made a Leopard Man, a satyr-like creature both ape and goat and several creatures similar to wolves.

The narrator gradually realises that the experiments are not the worst of Moreau's cruelty:

> 'Before they had been beasts, their instincts fitly adapted to their surroundings, and happy as living things can be. Now they stumbled in the shackles of humanity, lived in a fear that never died, fretted by a law they could not understand; their mock human existence began in an agony, was one long internal

153

struggle, one long dread of Moreau – and for what? It was the wantonness that stirred me.'

The creatures begin to change back into animals, and take their revenge on Moreau. The narrator escapes and returns to civilisation, but finds it hard to adapt to mankind after beasts, for 'I could not persuade myself that the men and women I met were not also another, still passably human, Beast People, animals half-wrought into the outward image of human souls...'

This is a nightmare of a book, and anyone who respects animals will find it especially odious. Dr Moreau was possessed by a monstrous idea, in every sense, but are we all that much better? We eat animals, hunt them, cage them and make them perform tricks for us in circuses. Even worse are the experiments for which animals are used in the name of vivisection and medical research, and worst of all is the use of animals to test cosmetics – to make *us* look prettier and feel better. White rabbits have shampoo inserted in their eyes for 'irritation' tests, beagles are forced to smoke to test the effects of tobacco fumes and monkeys are subjected to intense noise and reared in isolation with parts of their brains removed. Can anything be more horrible than that?

Every week 100,000 animals die in British laboratories. This makes Dr Moreau look like an amateur, in spite of today's excuse that these deaths are 'in a good cause'.

And what about the dolphin, that wise and affectionate creature whose natural home is in the depths of the sea? He is kept in an American side-show in a tub little bigger than a large bath, with people staring and music blaring and neon-lights glaring through the day and night. *That* is true horror.

*Almost Human*

### The White Worm

*The Lair of the White Worm*, the novel by Bram Stoker, is one of the weirdest books ever written. It is also one of the funniest, partly because Stoker took it so seriously from start to finish. At the very least it is a literary curiosity, and one day it might well become a cult. Though it is little known, it is Stoker's most popular book after *Dracula*, and is frequently reprinted in paperback.

Adam Salton, a wealthy young Australian, returns to his ancestral home in the Peak District. He meets his neighbour, Lady Arabella March, at the start of the book when her carriage has broken down. He mends it, and then notices several black snakes slithering on the ground around him. Lady Arabella slips from her carriage 'with a quick gliding motion', and he cries out to warn her, but the snakes turn and wriggle away as fast as they can, apparently more scared of Lady Arabella than she is of them.

Is there something strange about Lady Arabella? Yes, there is. He takes a good look at her:

> 'She was clad in some kind of soft white stuff, which clung close to her form, showing to the full every movement of her sinuous figure. She wore a close-fitting cap of some fine fur of dazzling white. Coiled round her white throat was a large necklace of emeralds, whose profusion of colour dazzled when the sun shone on them. Her voice was peculiar, very low and sweet, and so soft that the dominant note was of sibilation. Her hands, too, were peculiar – long, flexible, white, with a strange movement as of waving gently to and fro.'

*Lady Arabella is an immense white worm!* The next time he meets her, Adam is carrying a mongoose which he has brought to get rid of the snakes. Lady Arabella walks towards him:

> 'Hitherto the mongoose had been quiet, like a playful affectionate kitten; but when the two got close, Adam was horrified to see the mongoose, in a state of the wildest fury, with every hair standing on end, jump from his shoulder and run towards Lady Arabella. It looked so furious and so intent on attack that he called out a warning:
> "Look out – look out! The animal is furious and means to attack."

She pulls out a revolver and pours shot after shot into the creature.

Adam then notices the body of a little girl by the roadside. She is dead, and he notices on her neck some marks that look like those of teeth.

Adam talks to a dear old friend of the family, Sir Nathaniel de Salis, who tells him of a local legend about a monster that lives underground – a great white worm. Just imagine if such a creature could assume human form! Sir Nathaniel mentions an incident in Lady Arabella's childhood when she wandered into a small wood at night and was found unconscious, having received a 'poisonous bite'. To everyone's surprise she recovered, but people noticed that she then developed 'a terrible craving for cruelty, maiming and injuring birds and small animals – even killing them. I have come to the conclusion,' he says, 'that the foul White Worm obtained control of her body, just as her soul was leaving its earthly tenement – that would explain the sudden revival of energy, the strange and inexplicable craving for maiming and killing.'

## Almost Human

Like Dracula, the Worm moves under cover of darkness. A few nights later the two men see an immense tower of snowy white, tall and thin, with the green light of her eyes above the trees as she glides through the wood, with the vast coils of her serpent's body below. The white effect is the reflection of china clay in the soil. They decide that she must be destroyed.

Adam plants dynamite and lightning blows up Lady Arabella's lair:

> 'From this [the worm-hole] the agonised shrieks were rising, growing ever more terrible with each second that passed. Some of these fragments were covered with scaled skin as of a gigantic lizard or serpent. Once in a sort of lull or pause, the seething contents of the hole rose, after the manner of a bubbling spring, and Adam saw part of the thin form of Lady Arabella forced to the top amid a mass of slime, and what looked as if it had been a monster torn into shreds. .... Corruption comes with startling rapidity to beings whose destruction has been due wholly or in part to lightning – the whole mass seemed to have become all at once corrupt! The whole surface of the fragments, once alive, was covered with insects, worms and vermin of all kinds. The sight was horrible enough, but with the awful smell added, was simply unbearable. The Worm's hole appeared to breathe forth death in its most repulsive form.'

Stoker describes Lady Arabella as having 'the strength and impregnability of a diplodocus', which was a vegetarian dinosaur. Does that make you think of a creature constantly in the news today – the Loch Ness Monster? Note that everyone accepts that 'Nessie' is female. Could she be Lady Arabella come to life again, all the pieces joined up like the great Worm of Lambton? Of course not. She might be a relative, though!

## The Black Cat

> 'One night, returning home much intoxicated from one of my haunts about town, I fancied that the cat avoided my presence. I seized him; when, in his fright at my violence, he inflicted a slight wound upon my hand with his teeth. The fury of a demon instantly possessed me. I knew myself no longer. My original soul seemed, at once, to take its flight from my body; and a more than fiendish malevolence, gin-nurtured, thrilled every fibre of my frame. I took from my waistcoat-pocket a pen knife, opened it, grasped the poor beast by the throat, and deliberately cut one of its eyes from the socket! I blush, I burn, I shudder while I pen the damnable atrocity.'

This is from *The Black Cat* (1843), one of the most famous stories of Edgar Allan Poe. But, like so many of Poe's stories (see Chapter 4), it is not just horror for horror's sake, but a study of a man's guilty conscience.

He hangs the wretched cat, but buys another. When he discovers that it too has one of its eyes missing, he grows to hate it even more than the first. But the cat has its revenge after the man kills his wife with an axe and bricks her body into a wall.

When the police come to investigate her disappearance, he shows them around with the utmost ease. He even raps on the wall with his cane, but a terrible cry comes from behind the bricks, 'quickly swelling into one long, loud, and continuous scream, utterly anomalous and inhuman – a howl – a wailing shriek, half of horror and half of triumph, such as might have arisen only out of hell . . .'

The police tear down the wall while the man staggers back. The corpse of his wife is revealed, greatly decayed and clotted with gore. 'Upon its head, with red extended mouth and solitary eye of fire, sat the hideous beast whose craft had seduced me into murder, and whose informing voice had consigned me to the hangman. I had walled the monster up within the tomb!'

*The Squaw*, by Bram Stoker, is another story in which a black cat has revenge. It concerns a character called – would you believe it – Elias P. Hutcheson, from Ismithian City, Bleeding Gulch, Maple Tree Country, Neb. On his travels he meets a young couple who are visiting Nuremberg Castle. Looking down from a parapet, he sees a cat playing with her kitten in the old moat twenty metres below them, and thinks he'll surprise them by dropping a pebble.

'You might hit the dear little thing,' the wife protests.

'Not me, ma'am,' says Elias P. 'Why, I'm as tender as a Maine cherry-tree. Lord, bless ye – I wouldn't hurt the poor pooty little critter more'n I'd scalp a baby. An' you may bet your variegated socks on that.'

But his joke misfires. The stone does not land beside them as intended – it plumps on the kitten's head, shattering its brains on the ground:

'The black cat cast a swift upward glance, and we saw her eyes like green fire fixed an instant on Elias P. Hutcheson; and then her attention was given to the kitten, which lay still with just a quiver of her tiny limbs, whilst a thin red stream trickled from a gaping wound. With a muffled cry, such as a human being might give, she bent over the kitten licking its wounds and moaning. Suddenly she seemed to realise that it was dead, and again threw her eyes up at us. I shall never forget the sight, for she looked the perfect incarnation of hate. Her green eyes blazed with lurid fire, and the white, sharp teeth seemed to almost shine through the blood which dabbled her mouth and whiskers. She gnashed her teeth, and her claws stood out stark and at full length on every paw. Then she made a wild rush up the wall as if to reach us, but when the momentum ended fell back, and further added to her horrible appearance for she fell on the kitten, and rose with her black fur smeared with its brains and blood.'


The visitors try to forget the incident and move inside the castle, the black cat stalking them below. They have come especially to see the torture chamber. This contains an unusual torture machine, the Iron Maiden or 'Squaw' of the title, shaped like a human being but with one half which swings open. When closed, a series of sharp spikes puncture the unfortunate victim trapped inside. The American is fascinated and insists on placing himself inside it, while the aged guide works the engine that closes the murderous door 'with a deliberate and excruciating slowness'. The Englishman's wife starts to faint, and when he has looked after her he glances up and notices the black cat crouching in the darkness.


'Her green eyes shone like danger lamps in the gloom of the place, and their colour was heightened by the blood which still smeared her coat and reddened her mouth. I cried out:

"The cat! look out for the cat!" for even then she sprang out before the engine. At this moment she looked like a triumphant demon. Her eyes blazed with ferocity, her hair bristled out till she seemed twice her normal size and her tail lashed about as does a tiger's when the quarry is before it. Elias P. Hutcheson when he saw her was amused, and his eyes positively sparkled with fun.'

But the cat does not leap at the Iron Maiden as we expect:

'... but straight at the face of the custodian. Her claws seemed to be tearing wildly as one sees in the Chinese drawings of the dragon rampant, and as I looked I saw one of them light on the poor man's eye, and actually tear through it and down his cheek, leaving a wide band of red where the blood seemed to spurt from every vein. With a yell of sheer terror which came quicker than even his sense of pain, the man leaped back, dropping as he did so the rope which held the iron door. I jumped for it, but was too late, for the cord ran like lightning through the pulley-block, and the heavy mass fell forward from its own weight.

As the door closed I caught a glimpse of our poor companion's face. He seemed frozen with terror. His eyes stared with a horrible anguish as if dazed, and no sound came from his lips.

And then the spikes did their work.'

The story ends with a gruesome touch – the cat sitting

on the American's head, purring as she licks the blood which trickles from the sockets of his eyes. 'I think no one will call me cruel,' says the Englishman, 'because I seized one of the executioner's old swords and shore her in two as she sat.'

Yet one has a sneaking sympathy for the cat, if only because of Elias P. Hutcheson's murder of the English language – 'bet your variegated socks' indeed!

# 7
# YOUR GUIDE TO HORROR

'The eyes were the worst. It was not my imagination. They were in truth like the eyes of a dead man, not blind but staring unfocused, unseeing.'

(*The Magic Island* by William Seabrook)

## Haiti – home of the Zombie

Across the Atlantic from West Africa, where the Leopard Men practised witchcraft, lies the island of Voodoo – Haiti.

African slaves were sent there, when it was a French colony, by King Louis the Thirteenth. He gave slave-rights to his colonists, and they tried to convert the heathen African to the Catholic Church.

Slaves came from four parts of Western Africa, most from the Congo. Transported to a strange island, they brought their superstitions and worshipped the ancestors they left behind in the African forests. In Haiti their primitive religion became Voodoo. It was banned to begin with, but forced into secrecy it became even stronger and more sinister. It was an explosive situation, for the French masters treated their slaves abominably, cutting off their hands for a trivial offence.

The first slaves arrived around 1650. Selling them was big business, and a hundred years later as many as 30,000 slaves were landed in Haiti every year. As one generation replaced another, a terrible yearning set in for the past, and the first revolutionary attempt at African independence took place in Haiti in 1757, led by Macandal, a slave from Guinea. Escaping from his plantation, he led a rebellion of fanatical fugitives, but he was captured and burnt to death. Several revolts followed until Dessalines proclaimed Haitian independence in 1804.

As Catholicism departed with the French colonists, Voodoo was established as the new religion. Voodoo was thrilling. It celebrated the past with the rhythmic beat of African drums, driving the dancers into such a state of frenzy that they collapsed – a sort of mass hysteria. Blood was essential for ceremonies – usually the sacrifice of such animals as pigs or hens, but occasionally of the 'hornless goat' or human being. There was a famous case in 1863 when a small girl was strangled at a New Year's ceremony, then cut up, and her flesh eaten along with other ritual foods. The next year eight Haitians were publicly executed for eating another girl. Such stories of cannibalism were rare, but they gave Haiti a bad name that has been hard to shake off.

Voodoo ceremonies took place in *tonnelles* – rough huts with mud floors in a back street out of town. They were conducted by Houngans, priests who practised both Wanga (black magic) and bush medicine, either with the medicinal use of leaves or with the use of poison. The Houngans were able to summon up spirit gods, and these could take possession of the dancers. When the spirit god was the ancient Papa Legba, the dancer became old and lame and the others would run forward with sticks and crutches to help him. The African God Agassa, half-panther, half-woman, made the possessed dancers stiffen their fingers into claws. Evil spirits threw the dancers into convulsions. Possession could last several hours and was sometimes so strong that the Haitians could walk on burning coals or hold their hands in boiling water without flinching. It was this atmosphere that created the Zombie, the living dead of the West Indies.

All Haitians were brought up to believe in stories of werewolves and black magic. They were probably the most superstitious people on earth. They believed that a sorcerer could dig up a grave before the body had time to rot, and lead the corpse away to become his servant. This was a Zombie. The peasants took every possible precaution against this, such as sowing up the corpse's mouth or filling it with earth, to stop it answering if the sorcerer called;

they also piled stones on top of the grave and guarded it carefully until the body had rotted.

How do you recognise a Zombie? By his glassy-eyed stare and nasal twang. He is obedient until he is given salt – this releases him, and is the basis of the most interesting case-history recorded by William Seabrook, an American writer and expert on the subject. In 1918, peasants were needed for work in the canefields. Conscripted in various ways, they poured into the area. One old headman, known as Colombier, led a band of ragged, shuffling creatures. They seemed dazed by their new surroundings and frightened by the noise and smoke of the factories, but became more subdued when they reached the canefields and started to work. To subdue them further, Colombier beat them and stole their wages.

Colombier's wife, Croyance, felt sorry for the Zombies, especially in the evening when they sat around dumbly, eating the tasteless food that was their compulsory diet, without any enjoyment. After several months there was a local fête, and as Colombier was away she acted on a sudden impulse and led the Zombies there as a treat. But they sat down in their usual stupor, seeing nothing.

Croyance now made her fatal mistake. She bought some biscuits to cheer them up, but unknown to her they were made from ground, *salted* peanuts. As they nibbled their biscuits, all their senses returned and they gave a cry of anguish, knowing they were dead.

They walked into the sunlight, a grim procession as they stumbled back to their native village. As they entered it, they were recognised by relatives and friends, who quickly spread the news of their return. Wives, children, fathers and mothers wept with happiness as they saw them, but the Zombies shuffled on sightlessly. A mother screamed and fell at her daughter's feet, but the girl walked over her.

When they reached their former graves, the Zombies began to claw at the stones. The moment they touched the earth of their former resting place they collapsed and, within a moment, were little more than rotting flesh. Their families buried them for the second time, then lay in ambush for Colombier and cut off his head when he passed.

Unlike the vampire or the werewolf, it is likely that some creature called the Zombie does exist. Certainly the Haitians believed in Zombies themselves, but more than 95 per cent of them remained in a primitive state of ignorance right up to the present day. If they believed that 'fire-hags' could hang up their skins at home and set fire to the canefields, if they believed in the vampire who sucked the blood of children and whose hair turned red in consequence, or in the werewolf that took the form of a dog, killing lambs and sometimes babies, then it is hardly surprising if they believed in Zombies too.

The question remains: what really is a Zombie? William Seabrook helps to answer with this description of a Zombie he met: 'The eyes were the worst. It was not my imagination. They were in truth like the eyes of a dead man, not blind but staring unfocused, unseeing.' He remembered the face of a dog he had seen in a laboratory in Columbia. The entire front brain of the animal had been removed in an operation, and although it was still alive, its eyes were like those of the Zombie. He spoke, but there was no response. Suddenly he was certain that Zombies were nothing more than 'poor ordinary demented human beings, idiots forced to toil in the fields.'

But the most convincing definition of the Zombie is the official statement, Article 246 in the old Penal Code of

Haiti, which explains the transformation of Man into Zombie:

> 'Also to be termed intention to kill, by poisoning, is *the use of substances* whereby a person is not killed but reduced to *a state of lethargy*, more or less prolonged, and this without regard to the manner in which the substances were used or what were their later result. If following the state of lethargy the person is buried, then the attempt will be termed murder.'

What substances? Obviously the skilful use of drugs, probably made from local plants which we know nothing about.

A Voodoo trance could last for several days, in which the Zombie went about his work hardly realising it. Obviously it was very useful for the boss to have such a willing, uncomplaining slave. This was the motive for supplying the Zombie with drugs. He could move, eat, hear and even speak, but had no memory of his past or knowledge of his present, hideous condition. He was little more than a beast of burden reduced by drugs to a state almost indistinguishable from death.

In Haiti today, Voodoo has been reduced to a tourist attraction for the entertainment of foreigners. But this means it is still practised. Who knows what undercurrents linger beneath the jolly surface of tourism...?

**The Place of Dread**
This is the northern tip of Makin-Meang, the northernmost island of the Gilberts in the Central Pacific. It is described in Arthur Grimble's excellent study of primitive life – *A Pattern of Islands* (1952).

## Your Guide to Horror

Grimble heard weird stories about the ghosts of Makin-Meang before he went there as District Officer. It was regarded by the Gilbertese as a halfway stop between the living and the dead. Anyone who died on the Gilberts had to go to the north of this island if he wanted to continue to paradise, and had to pass Nakaa, the Watcher at the Gate.

If he died on one of the other fifteen Gilbert Islands he took the western path to the north, but the ghosts of local people took the eastern side. Either route was all right for the living islanders when they travelled north, for they were going *with* the stream of the ghosts, provided they never, ever looked back. The danger lay in the return journey. Then it was vital to take the emptier, eastern route, and find out beforehand if anyone had died that day. If you met a ghost face to face, you were done for.

Grimble asked the Native Magistrate to find him a guide who would take him to the Place of Dread. The Magistrate yielded against his will, supplying him with a giant of a man, a local constable, who would act as guide. This man warned Grimble not to look back as they took the road north, because if he did so, and saw a ghost, he would die within the year.

So they set off, carrying a large seed-coconut as a gift to plant in Nakaa's grove. Grimble, as a stranger on his first visit, had to carry it, and suspected that the constable had deliberately picked a heavy one. They reached the Place of Dread, which was 'merely a blazing acre or two of coral rock,' and planted the coconut. By now Grimble was desperately thirsty and asked his guide for a drink of coconut milk. The man was horrified – he said the trees belonged to Nakaa and could not be touched.

So they started the dry journey back along the eastern coast, the constable keeping a sullen forty paces behind,

Grimble's thirst was so bad that he decided at that point to ignore the guide and ask anyone he met, anywhere, to pick him a nut from the top of a tree. And then, across the curving beach ahead, he saw a figure coming towards him. 'My eyes never left him, because my intent was pinned on his getting me that drink.' The man drew closer. He walked with a limp, and was a grizzled man of fifty or so, dressed rather ceremoniously. As he came up, Grimble noticed that his left cheek was scarred from the jawbone to the temple.

But did the man see him? To Grimble's astonishment he passed by and continued on his journey as if Grimble did not exist: 'I was shocked speechless. It was so grossly unlike the infallible courtesy of the islanders.'

Then he thought the man might be a lunatic. He called out to the constable to stop him, so he could find out who he was. But the constable did not seem to hear, probably because of the sound of the surf, and ignored the man as he passed by.

Grimble ran back to him. 'Who is that man?' he asked. The constable stopped, bewildered. Then, as Grimble repeated his question, sweat broke out on his forehead. "I am afraid in this place!" he screamed high in his head, like a woman, and, without another word, he bolted out on the beach with an arm guarding his eyes.'

When Grimble arrived at the house of the Native Magistrate, he found the constable on the verandah. Grimble told the Magistrate what had happened and described the stranger who had passed by so rudely. He mentioned the limp and the scar. The Native Magistrate exchanged nods with the constable. 'That was indeed Na Biria,' he murmured. Grimble asked to see the man, only to be told:

'He is dead. He died this afternoon, soon before three o'clock.'

Grimble stood there dumbfounded. Suddenly he saw Na Biria, at the moment of death, projecting his dying thought, with sixty generations of fear behind it, along that eastern road to the Place of Dread. 'Had I received the impact of his thought as it passed my way? Or if not, what was it I had seen?'

If the man had died at three, he would not yet be buried. Grimble demanded to see his body. The constable was frightened by the idea, but the Magistrate was a Christian (who should know better than to believe in such things) and told Grimble to follow him. They heard the mourners a hundred metres away. They were beating the walls with sticks, to frighten away strange ghosts. Seeing them so earnestly at work, Grimble recovered his sense of decency. 'These folk believed utterly in what they were doing. For them, the dead man's whole eternity depended on their ritual. For them, the intrusion of me, a stranger, would send him to certain strangulation in Nakaa's net.' He turned away and the Native Magistrate followed him in silence.

Of course Grimble was right, but the questions he leaves behind are tantalising – would he have recognised the corpse? Would he have had a scar on his left cheek? Was he the limping man on the beach?

If so, he would have had certain proof of thought transference at the moment of death.

### The horror of Glamis
Guide books might say, and probably do, that the Scottish castle of Glamis in Count Angus is 'steeped in history'.

References to Glamis (which is pronounced 'glarms') go back for more than a thousand years, and it was here that Shakespeare's Macbeth – if not the real one – welcomed King Duncan under his battlements and murdered him.

More recently, Princess Margaret was born here, for this is the seat of the Earls of Strathmore and the Queen Mother is part of that family.

Legends are rampant – they include the story of an Earl Beardie who played cards with the Devil, the bloodstains of King Malcolm II in the room where he was murdered in the eleventh century, which never rub out, a tongueless woman who looks out from a barred window, and a ghostly Black Boy who sits beside the door leading to the Queen Mother's sitting-room and is said to have been a servant here two hundred years ago. There is even a vampire – a woman who was locked up and left to die when she was found sucking the blood of a victim. As vampires cannot be destroyed except in the ritual way, it might still be there.

Certainly *something* seems to be in Glamis castle. Sir Walter Scott started the most horrific legend of all when he referred to a secret room known only to the Earls of Strathmore. They refuse to discuss it with anyone, except the heir who is told the dark secret on his twenty-first birthday.

This haunted chamber is supposed to have been walled up when the Ogilvy Clan, pursued by the Lindsays, asked for refuge at the Castle. Showing a strange form of hospitality, the Earl of Strathmore felt he could not refuse them, but once inside he locked them in a far room and left them to starve to death. Many years afterwards a later Earl was disturbed by such curious wailings one night that he went the next morning to investigate – when the wall was broken down he collapsed from the stench and the sight of the skeletons, some of whom appeared to have eaten themselves in a struggle to stay alive.

Another explanation for the Haunted Room is that a

monster was born into the family two hundred years ago, so hideous and deformed that it had to be kept hidden. Rumours even suggested you would go mad if you set eyes on 'it'. In spite of the deformity, the creature lived to an incredible age, far beyond 150 years, and some people claim it is still alive. It was known as 'The horror of Glamis'.

Could this be true? Hard to say while the family keep silent, but one Earl was said to be furious when he returned from an outing to find that his guests had gone into every room in the castle and hung towels from the windows. When they went outside they noticed that several windows remained unmarked, suggesting walled-up rooms behind them. Lady Granville, the elder sister of the Queen Mother, once said: 'We were never allowed to talk about it when we were children ... my father and grandfather absolutely refused to discuss it.' The present Earl told the author: I fear I have no information whatever as to the existence of 'A Monster' now or in the past.'

Let us accept the word of one of the former Earls: 'If you could know of it, you would thank God you were not me.'

## Whitby

If you go to Whitby on the Yorkshire coast, take a copy of Bram Stoker's *Dracula* with you. Few towns in England have changed so little since the 1890s when Stoker stayed here.

Whitby lies in a valley, cut in half by the River Esk, and part of its charm lies in the fishing port that is still busy in the harbour. Walk across the bridge that links the two sides of the town, past a cluster of fine old houses, and up the 199 stone steps known as the Church Stairs to St Mary's Church with the ruined Abbey behind. After such a climb, you may be glad to sit on one of the wooden benches in the graveyard. Compare the place in *Dracula* and you will find it exactly as Stoker described it, give or take a few cars and the sound of a Bingo hall's loudspeaker drifting across the valley. The magnificent sepia prints by the great Victorian photographer Sutcliffe (1853-1941), exhibited in the town, confirm how little has changed.

The graveyard is extraordinary. Most of the tombstones have kept their shape, though salt winds have worn away the lettering and darkened the stone. They stand in high wild grass like black lines of surf. There is an appropriate atmosphere of neglect, which appealed to Bram Stoker: 'This is, to my mind, the nicest spot in Whitby, for it lies right over the town, and has a full view of the harbour and all up to the bay to where the headland called Kettleness stretches into the sea.' This is from 'Mina Murray's Journal' (a passage in *Dracula*), but plainly echoes Stoker's own feelings. 'There are walks with seats beside them, through the churchyard; and people go and sit there all day long . . .'

This is the place where Dracula came to England, when his ship with the great boxes of earth and the dead captain lashed to the wheel was hurled ashore in a great storm. There was no sign of life aboard except for a great dog that leapt on to the sands and bounded up the cliff towards the graveyard. This was Dracula!

You can see the elegant curve of East Crescent from the wooden benches, and it was from her window there that Mina Murray (Jonathan Harker's fiancée) looked out in the evening in the hope of seeing her friend Lucy in her favourite seat, after Lucy had disappeared:

'Then as the cloud passed I could see the ruins of the Abbey coming into view; and as the edge of a narrow band of light as sharp as a sword-cut moved along, the church and the churchyard became gradually visible. Whatever my expectation was, it was not disappointed, for there on our favourite seat, the silver light of the moon struck a half-reclining figure, snowy white. The coming of the cloud was too quick for me to see much, for shadow shut down on light almost immediately; but it seemed to me as though something dark stood behind the seat where the white figure shone, and bent over it. What is was, whether man or beast, I could not tell.'

Mina hurries across the valley, down the narrow streets and up the steep steps:

'My knees trembled and my breath became laboured as I toiled up the endless steps to the Abbey. I must have gone fast, and yet it seemed to me as if my feet were weighted with lead and as though every joint in my body was rusty. When I got almost to the top I could see the seat and the white figure. I called in fright – "Lucy! Lucy!" – and something raised a head and from where I was I could see a white face and red gleaming eyes...'

Mina barefoot and Lucy in her night-dress, they scurry down the steps and through the back lanes to the safety of the Crescent. But Dracula's fangs have claimed their first victim in Britain and poor Lucy is doomed.

## Transylvania

Yes, there is such a place! It is not a fantasy land dreamt up by a film company, like Ruritania, but a state in Northern Romania near the borders of Hungary. It is much as Stoker described it in *Dracula* in 1897, and this is remarkable because he never set foot there himself. He gained his research from a Baedeker's guide, books in the British Museum, and information from his Hungarian friend, Professor Arminius Vambery.

It is strange to stand today in Bistrita – called Bistritz in the novel – where Jonathan Harker stayed the night before he left for Castle Dracula. Unlike many of Romania's cities, which are extremely modern, Bistrita is pleasantly old-fashioned. There is a delightful restaurant with a local orchestra, rich in atmosphere, and a small wooden hotel that could have been the model for Stoker's Golden Krone; for good measure there is a coffin-maker's opposite. Now a big modern hotel has been completed, deliberately named The Golden Crown to please Dracula-minded visitors.

Leaving Bistrita, you enter the Borgo Pass. It is splendid, rolling countryside. No wonder Jonathan Harker lost his 'ghostly fears in the beauty of the scene' as he drove through it. He referred to 'a green sloping land full of forests and woods, with here and there steep hills, crowned with clumps of trees or with farmhouses . . .' It is all there still – the huts with wood-shingled roofs, orchards of plums, solitary stone crosses by the roadside, and the occasional figure of a shepherd – when you can see them all in the white mists that swirl around.

One thing is missing – Castle Dracula. It belonged to Stoker's imagination alone, and that is the problem. Ever since one of the major world airlines started 'A Tour Package with a Toothy Grin – an 18 day fully-escorted romp through middle Europe called "Spotlight on Dracula", Dracula Tours have flown in from all over the world. Tourists expect to see Castle Dracula and the places Stoker wrote about, but are shown the wrong Dracula instead!

## Your Guide to Horror

British tourists booked on the recent 'Dracula Tours' arranged by a British airline company have seen fascinating parts of southern Romania but they haven't gone near Transylvania. Instead they have been shown the fortresses of the historical Dracula, Vlad the Impaler (see Chapter 8). Instead of Castle Dracula, visitors are led around Bran Castle – sort of 'stand-in'. You hear the word 'Dracula' whispered by the guides constantly, but Bran has little to do with Vlad Dracula and nothing whatever to do with Stoker's Count.

This placed the Romanian government in a dilemma. To begin with they did not want their national hero, Vlad, labelled as a ghoul and vampire. Stoker's novel has never been translated into Romanian, and at first they could not understand what all the fuss was about. Gradually they realised they have a tourist gold-mine on their back doorstep. Consequently, they are proposing to direct the Dracula tours to the north, and build a Castle Dracula especially. They are thinking big. With tapes of wolves howling along the Borgo Pass, a caleche with four coal-black horses to take passengers on their final stage of the fearful journey, bats on wires and waitresses with fangs serving the appropriate food and drink (red wine, of course), it could be a triumph – a horror version of Disneyland.

Meanwhile, the only visitors who see the Dracula-landscape of Stoker's novel are independent travellers or those who have joined the Dracula Society on their recent tours in which they covered 1600 kilometres in twelve days. Bernard Davies, the Honorary Secretary, wrote after such a holiday:

> 'The trip was simply magnificent. I don't know what the others were expecting, but the journey came up to my expectations all the way. The Romanians pulled

out all the stops to give us a good time and really entered into the spirit of the thing. The hospitality was terrific, especially the Jonathan Harker luncheon at Bistrita ('roast beef of outlaws' and 'butcher's meat with pepper' on the menu), which developed into the most gigantic binge lasting (I think) until about two in the morning. What a day! . . . Beautiful cloudless weather either end; just two days in the middle round the Borgo Pass appropriately dark and stormy, and when we picnicked up in the Călimani Mountains round a big fire . . . it actually snowed on us. We even managed to have a fight with a band of gypsies! It simply was the most amazing experience. How Bram Stoker would have envied us the actuality of Transylvania!'

## Borley Rectory

A dull, depressing, dismal place, this Suffolk rectory, 97 kilometres from London, was built in 1863 by the Reverend Henry Bull. It would be of no importance except for the overwhelming evidence that it was, and perhaps still is, haunted. Harry Price, the famous ghost hunter who founded the National Laboratory of Psychical Research, made various tests before his death in 1948 and called it 'the most haunted house in England'.

The ghost, rather obviously, was a nun. Story had it that she tried to elope with a coachman and was walled up alive in a convent that used to exist nearby. A canon of Carlisle Cathedral claimed that she was a French nun called Marie Lairre, who had eloped with her lover to England and been killed by him and buried in the cellar of the house that stood there before Borley Rectory. When a subsequent excavation unearthed human remains, some people thought they were those of Marie.

Harry Price started his investigations in 1929, when the new tenants, the Reverend and Mrs Smith, wrote to a newspaper complaining of poltergeist activity in the form of doorbells ringing at night, keys pushed out of locks and general annoyance. Mrs Smith heard whisperings that sounded something like 'Don't Carlos, don't.'

Price saw the nun in the garden, and the Smiths moved out. The Reverend and Mrs Foyster moved in, and the poltergeists hated them! Young Mrs Foyster was thrown out of bed, locked in her room, and nearly smothered by a mattress. Scribbles appeared on the walls, apparently addressed to her – 'Marianne' – asking for prayers and Mass to be said. Mrs Foyster answered underneath: 'I cannot understand, please tell me more', but it seems highly probable that she had written these messages herself, either subconsciously or deliberately because she hated the place and wanted to leave.

The Foysters moved out in 1935 and so did the next rector, allowing Harry Price to rent Borley Rectory for a year. He moved in with forty-eight voluntary amateur psychical detectives, but the results were most disappointing – nothing happened! In 1939 the Rectory was burnt to the ground.

These are the facts, as related by Frank Smyth in his book on *Ghosts and Poltergeists*. He admits that many experts regarded Price with suspicion:

> 'A *Daily Mail* reporter described how he had caught Price in the act of manufacturing phenomena during the 1929 investigations. His story prompted Mrs Smith, wife of the former rector, to state that she and

her husband had never believed the place to be haunted by anything other than rats.'

Mrs Smith continually changed her story. More damaging was a book *The Haunting of Borley Rectory* (1956) by three psychical researchers, who accused Price of suppressing facts when they did not suit him, and blowing them up when they did.

'They pointed to the acoustic data on the Rectory (writes Smyth) indicating that most of the auditory phenomena (the sound effects) could be attributed to natural causes. They leaned heavily on the probable involvement of Marianne Foyster in the poltergeist activity ... By the time the authors had finished scrutinizing all the evidence, Borley's reputation as the "most haunted house in England", and Price's reputation as ghost hunter were largely shattered. Since then, other psychical researchers have tackled the Borley case and formed various opinions about it. Even today, it remains one of the most debated of all ghost stories.'

But Smyth is quick to credit Price's detective work in other cases.

Peter Underwood, President of the Ghost Club, has interviewed practically everyone connected with Borley and was originally invited to join the Ghost Club by Price himself. He probably knows more about Borley than anyone alive and has no doubts: 'Borley Rectory really was the most haunted house in England, as far as I am concerned – so much happened there over a long period of time.'

Though he says there is no historical evidence for the romantic story of the bricked-up nun, Peter Underwood confirms that a nun has been sighted constantly by different people, usually on 28th July. It was seen on the Nun's Walk, bordering the lawn, by four of the Reverend Bull's fourteen children on 28th July, 1900:

> 'As they reached the rectory gate, the three girls saw a nun-like figure gliding slowly along the Nun's Walk. The face of the figure was not visible and they heard no sound, but the figure appeared to be solid and substantial. After watching for a moment one of the sisters ran into the house and fetched an older sister; she joined the others and the four of them watched the rather frightening figure which half-glided and half-walked, soundlessly and purposelessly with bowed head along the edge of their lawn. Deciding that it must be a visiting nun telling her beads, the elder girl went forward with the intention of offering her some refreshment, whereupon the figure vanished: one moment it was there and the next it was gone. There was no shaking the testimony of the Bull sisters on this experience, and I heard the story from Ethel's lips on several occasions.'

It turned out later that their parents had also seen the ghost, ten years earlier on 28th July, but had decided not to tell the children in case they were alarmed. Another eyewitness, an elderly schoolmaster, told Peter Underwood that he had seen the nun several times, as early as 1886. The last sighting of the ghostly nun in the area where Borley Rectory once stood was in 1972.

### Highgate cemetery, London
A wonderfully eerie spot, even on a bright sunny morning.

The cemetery is divided into two parts, and though most people flock to the lower half to see the massive monument to Karl Marx, the north is more mysterious.

Highgate cemetery was designed by the foremost Victorian architects and landscape gardeners, with arches and steps and graceful avenues for the mourning families to walk through. It contains 100,000 tombs, so it is full now. It was a noble concept, but the northern part is so overgrown that foxes prowl through the woods at night and more than twenty varieties of bird live in the undergrowth. This makes it sound romantic, and it is, except that many of the graves have been broken into and tombstones overturned as if a legion of vampires has risen up and heaved them aside.

In fact people have claimed that they saw a huge vampire hovering over the graves. One hundred vampire hunters invaded the cemetery on 13th March, 1970, and vandalised the tombs. One unfortunate man, who parked his car nearby, returned in the morning to find a headless body propped against the steering-wheel!

The leading vampire hunter, and self-styled High Priest of the Occult Society, was jailed in 1974. He was charged with entering catacombs in consecrated ground ('Capers among the Catacombs' as one newspaper described it) and offering indignity to the remain of a body 'to the great scandal and disgrace of religion, decency and morality.' Police found salt scattered around his room at home and a wooden cross under his pillow, and claimed that voodoo dolls with pins in them had been posted to possible police witnesses against him. He was released in the summer of 1976, claiming that he had held witchcraft ceremonies inside the jail ('there was a flourishing coven when I left'). At least he vowed never to stalk Highgate again. This is just as well, for the place needs all the help it can receive in the struggle against weeds, neglect and such publicity. It was closed temporarily in April 1975, but has now been reopened and a society called 'The Friends of Highgate' are doing their best to restore it to a reasonable condition.

# 8 REAL HORRORS

'My knife is nice and sharp I want to get to work right away if I get a chance. Good luck.
Yours truly,
Jack the Ripper'

(letter to a newspaper, 1888)

**Countess Bathory**

She was possibly the cruellest woman ever to have lived. No one is sure how many women she killed, but estimates hover around six hundred. Born in 1560, she was the widow of a Hungarian nobleman, Count Nadasay. She was brought to trial in 1611 after so many girls had vanished near her castle that the villagers demanded a search.

The governor of the province, her own cousin, the village priest and a number of soldiers raided the castle and arrested everyone inside. They found – quite literally – a bloodbath. One girl was found in the hall, dead and drained of blood, and many others in the dungeons.

The Countess, as close to a vampire as a real person can get, had drunk their blood in the vain belief that this helped the complexion. She bathed in blood too, but these horrible beauty baths failed to work. A cage had been built, rather like Bram Stoker's *Squaw* (see Chapter 6) – a version of the Iron Maiden, with a series of spikes that pierced the skin as it closed on the girl inside in a tight embrace. The Countess Bathory would sit underneath enjoying the shower of blood that rained down.

She refused to attend her trial, and because of her importance the lawyers were undecided how to punish her, though her servants were put to death. Finally King Mathias of Hungary ordered her imprisonment in the castle, where she died three years later. The Lord Palantine described her as 'the blood-thirsty and blood sucking Godless woman'.

**Gilles de Rais**

He was an earlier counterpart. He was brought to trial in 1440 for the torture of children, most of them boys, and was executed. He, too, was obsessed by the idea of blood, yet he was a Marshall of France and a brave soldier in the

Hundred Years War. He was thought by some to be the original 'Bluebeard'.

## Dracula – Prince Vlad V of Wallachia

There *was* such a person! He was a brave warrior and is considered a national hero in Romania today, but he was cruel even for his own time (1431–76). To give one example, he visited one of his strongholds and invited all the beggars in the town to a grand feast. Naturally they were overjoyed and crowded into the great hall. Then he locked the doors and set fire to the place. He explained that he wanted to reduce the risk of plague.

His enemies were the Turks and it is claimed that after one battle in 1456 he killed 20,000 of them. After another victory over the heathen Turk, the bells of Christendom rang out in rejoicing as far as the island of Rhodes. It was said that he made his state of Wallachia so safe that it was possible to leave a purse in the middle of the road and no one would touch or steal it. Probably no one *dared* to touch it!

In 1458, Vlad Dracula built the citadel of Bucharest, the present capital of Romania. His main headquarters were in Tirgoviste, where tourists are taken today on the *wrong* Dracula Tour (thinking they are going to see the landscape of Stoker's Count Dracula). It is well worth seeing all the same – the ruined battlements of Vlad's former palace dominated by a sixteenth century tower with a magnificent view of the town, and flocks of schoolchildren below, in tunics of blue and white, listening while their teacher tells them about the glories of Vlad Dracula, if not the gore!

He was known in his day as Vlad the Impaler (Vlad Tepes, *tzepa* meaning spike) because he enjoyed impaling his enemies on tall stakes – an agonising torture as the man's weight forced the sharpened point slowly upwards, splitting him apart. After several hours, the man died – seldom can death have been so welcome. An old print shows Vlad munching a lunch beneath a row of impaled Turks as if it were the most natural thing in the world. When one of his men was rash enough to object to the screams and smells, Vlad had him impaled as well, on a higher stake, saying: 'You live up there, yonder, where the stench cannot reach you.'

To be fair to Vlad, the thousands of impaled bodies dotted across the countryside acted as a terrible warning to the Turks not to invade any further. There was a famous episode when a deputation of visiting ambassadors forgot to doff their turbans to Vlad in respect. He ordered the turbans should be nailed to their heads – a lesson in good manners to be copied later by Ivan the Terrible.

Was Vlad Dracula the model for Count Dracula? Some people think so, including members of the Dracula Society in London. As a matter of fact, there is a resemblance in the 1485 'Lubeck print' of Vlad to the 'thin nose and peculiarly arched nostrils', the 'heavy moustache' and the 'peculiarly sharp white teeth' that Stoker gives to the Count in the novel. He mentions some of the historical background too. That's as far as the resemblance goes, for Vlad was *not* a vampire. Most probably, Stoker gave a cry of delight when he heard the name of Drac-ula, which rolls so menacingly around the tongue, and learnt all he could about the historical ruler who was also known as 'son of the devil' and 'son of the dragon'. Stoker's imagination did the rest.

## Ivan the Terrible

Tsar of Russia, he lived from 1530 to 1584 and was given to fits of mad anger and prayerful repentance. In one of the former he murdered his eldest son. The young man was tactless enough to taunt his father over his losses abroad to the Poles. Ivan saw red – maybe literally – and struck his son again and again on the head with a heavy steel handle. With his last words, the young Tsar forgave his father. He was given a great state funeral in Moscow.

Ivan shared Vlad's love of torture. Once he attacked a castle for several days with cannon until the people inside decided on a last heroic act. They filled the vaults with gunpowder, and one of the defenders took a lighted torch to blow up the castle and everyone in it, so that they should not fall into Ivan's hands. There was a terrific explosion, and everyone perished except for the man who started it. He lived for a short time but was dead when his blackened body was hoisted on a stake to be impaled. Ivan was so angry that he murdered all the other inhabitants, cutting them to bits or burning them alive. After such atrocities, there is no need to ask how he got his name!

### Rasputin

Grigori Yefimovich Rasputin (1872–1916) has been called 'the mad monk', 'the holy Devil' and other such names. He has been portrayed in films as a wild, black-bearded peasant whose scandals and intrigues brought about the downfall of Nicholas and Alexandra, the Tsar and Tsarina of Russia.

Rasputin possessed remarkable powers of healing by touch. As the Tsar's little boy suffered from haemophilia (a condition which makes it difficult to stop bleeding once it starts, so that even a scratch is dangerous), it is hardly surprising that the Tsarina was desperately anxious for any help Rasputin might offer.

Was he so evil? Christopher Lee, who portrayed him in

a film, thinks he has been 'much maligned'. So does Colin Wilson in his book *The Occult*. To start with, Wilson dismisses the claim that the very name 'rasputin' means 'the dirty one': 'If it did, he would no doubt have had the sense to change his name early in his career. It means a crossroads and happens to be as common as Smith in the village where he was born, Pokrovskoe.'

Rasputin was accused of meddling in Russian politics and wielding power over the Russian royal family. Wilson does not believe this. Perhaps people feared that Rasputin would use his influence politically, for he was murdered on 29th December, 1916. He was invited to a dinner party by Prince Yussipov, an aristocratic dandy. First he was given poisoned cakes, but these had no effect, possibly because he had been taking small amounts of cyanide for some time to make him immune. Then he was shot. As he staggered out of the house his attackers shot him again, terrified by his superhuman strength. Finally they beat him to death with an iron bar and stuck him under the ice in the River Neva that flows through Petrograd, or Leningrad as it is now called. Even then, scratches were found on the ice where he had tried to crawl out before he died.

Rasputin left a letter in which he forecast his own death and prophesied the end of the Russian royal family. He said that if he was killed by Russian noblemen the Tsar and his family would lose the throne within two years. The Russian Revolution took place the following year, and the Tsar, his wife and his children (with the possible exception of Anastasia) were executed in 1918.

Plainly Rasputin had extraordinary, almost hypnotic powers – but the evidence does not confirm that he was really the 'horror man' so often described.

## Sawney Bean, the Scottish cannibal

You only have to fly over Scotland to realise how surprisingly unspoilt some parts remain, even today. Imagine what it would have been like in remote regions a few hundred years ago, and the sort of dangers a traveller might meet.

Sawney Bean was born a few kilometres outside Edinburgh, in the reign of James I of Scotland. His father was a hedger and ditcher, and Sawney tried this too, but tired of it quickly. He ran off to a lonely part of the countryside, the coast of Galloway, where he lived for the next twenty-five years. During this time, he had a large number of children by the woman he had taken with him, and they gave him an even larger number of grand-children – not so much a family as a clan. Their home was a series of caves by the shore. Their supplies came from robbing passing travellers, and their food from eating them.

The limbs of victims were pickled, but at times they had so many that they threw them into the sea, as far from their caves as possible. When the tide washed up arms and legs along the coastline, people wondered who was guilty of such atrocities. As more and more travellers diappeared in this particular part of Scotland, the outcry grew. Spies were sent out, but either they returned with nothing to tell, or they were never seen again. Innocent people were executed, and many moved away before they were suspected. The countryside became increasingly desolate.

Meanwhile, the vast Sawney Bean family flourished. They were careful never to attack more than two horsemen at a time, and surrounded these carefully so there was no chance of a rapid escape. Travellers on foot were easier game – four or five at a time were disposed of easily and dragged to their caves. When the tide was high, the water came two hundred metres inside. The cave stretched for nearly two kilometres. No one, seeing such a place, would believe that people could live there.

Then, as it was bound to, their luck ran out. A man and wife were returning by horseback from a country fair, when they were attacked in the usual manner. The ferocity was described by John Nicholson in his *Historical Tales connected with the South of Scotland* (1843):

> 'In the conflict the poor woman fell from behind him, and was instantly butchered before her husband's face, for the female cannibals cut her throat, and fell to sucking her blood with as great a gust, as if it had been wine; this done, they ript up her belly, and pulled out all her entrails. Such a dreadful spectacle made the man make the more obstinate resistance, as he expected the same fate, if he fell into their hands.'

He fought back, and at that moment twenty or thirty men, also returning from the fair, arrived in time to rescue him. The man told them what had happened and showed them the body of his wife, which the Beans had dragged away and then abandoned. Shocked by their discovery, they took the man to Glasgow, where the magistrates instantly informed the King.

Four days later, the King set out in person with four hundred men, led by the only man who had survived such an attack by the cannibals. A team of bloodhounds went with them. Nothing was found. Even when they reached the mouth of the cave they could see nothing, and were continuing along the seashore when some of the hounds took up a scent and bounded inside. Immediately there was such a hideous howling that the soldiers turned back to investigate. All was darkness, but the hounds went deeper and deeper inside, refusing to come back as ordered. When the soldiers realised something or someone must be there, they sent for torches.

> 'Legs, arms, thighs, hands and feet of men, women and children, were hung up in rows, like dried beef; a great many limbs laid in pickle, and a great mass of money, both gold and silver, with watches, rings, swords, pistols and a large quantity of clothes, both linen and woolen, and an infinite number of other things which they had taken from those they had murdered, were thrown together in heaps or hung up against the sides of the den.'

They took all the human flesh they could find and buried it in the sand. Then they seized Sawney Bean and his wife, eight sons, six daughters, eighteen grandsons and fourteen granddaughters, and dragged them back to Edinburgh for all the countryside to see – the 'cursed tribe' captured at last.

They were executed at Leith without trial – it was not thought necessary. The men were dismembered and the rest burnt to death. 'They all in general died without the least signs of repentance, but continued cursing and vending the most dreadful imprecations to the very last gasp of life.'

## The Stranglers of Bombay

The religious assassins who terrorised this region of India in the nineteenth century gave a name to the English language – *thug*. This is defined by the Oxford Dictionary as 'cut-throat, ruffian'. The Thugs were also called Phansigars ('phansi' meaning noose), for these were The Stranglers of Bombay.

They were unusual criminals – deeply religious and frequently respected members of the community who enjoyed killing. When they robbed travellers it was not so much the theft as the strangulation that excited them, as they offered up their victims as sacrifice to the Hindu Goddess Kali.

In his psychology of murder, *Order of Assassins*, Colin Wilson describes their cunning method of attack. They lived quietly for most of the year in their villages, causing no suspicion, but in winter they took to the roads, making sure they kept at least 150 kilometres from home. When they came across a group of travellers, one or two of the Thugs would approach and ask if they could join them for protection. A few days later some more Thugs would do the same. Soon there were more Thugs than travellers. They waited for an evening when the travellers were seated round the fire, then three Thugs would creep up behind each victim. At a signal, one Thug would pass the strangling cloth round the traveller's neck, another grab his legs, and the third seize his hands or kneel on his back. It was all over in seconds. Then they hacked up the bodies so that they could not be identified. The legs were cut off and, if there was time, all the limbs were mutilated.

Now came the most important part for the Thugs – a private religious ceremony in which they prayed to Kali and ate the sacred *goor*, a sugary substance. One of the captured Thugs told an English army captain, William Sleeman, 'Let any man once taste of that *goor* and he will be a Thug, though he know all the trades and have all the wealth of the world.'

Sleeman was fascinated by the Thug atrocities and in

1829, when he revealed that they killed thousands of travellers every year, he caused a sensation both in India and back home in England. The next year Sleeman was given the job of suppressing them.

To begin with, the Thugs kept to a strict code of rules. Because Kali was a Goddess, no woman was supposed to be killed, nor blind man, nor carpenter. There were several such exceptions, but eventually this became so tiresome to the Thugs that they grew greedy and careless and no one was safe. On one occasion, after they had strangled twenty men and five women, they were going to take two young children with them. One boy cried so loudly for his murdered mother that the Thugs picked him up by his feet and dashed his brains out on a rock. They left him there and his body was found the next morning. Several of the Thugs were captured, and it was this sort of bungling, compared to the careful precautions they had used before, that proved their undoing. By 1850, 4000 Thugs had been brought to trial, and their thuggery was over.

Colin Wilson, also author of *The Occult*, is particularly interested in their compulsion to kill. They practised violence for the sake of violence, rather like the Manson killers of California in our own time. He writes:

> 'This exciting game – of stalking and strangling human beings – became a drug, an addiction. This is what troubled the British investigators, who were ordinary soldiers and civil servants – men of the Dr Watson type. They sensed that the Thug murders were an inverted creative act, which brought its own peculiar deep satisfaction, and the thought made them shudder.'

The fact that they murdered in the name of religion does not make them any the less horrible. On the contrary, it makes them worse.

## Jack the Ripper

His term of terror was short and swift and far from sweet. In 1888 he killed five women in six weeks in 'a square mile' of London streets. While Count Dracula is so familiar that he seems almost human, the Ripper – who *was* real – has become a part of folklore.

His fame (one could almost say his popularity) is as fascinating as the murders he committed. He caused a panic throughout all of England at the time. Today, nearly a hundred years later, a new book is published about him every year, Scotland Yard receives several 'Ripper' letters a week, tourists are guided round his old murder sites in the East End, and plays, films and even musicals continue to make his name a household word.

Why is Jack the Ripper the most celebrated murderer in history? There is one obvious reason – he escaped. London police or 'peelers' (some of them dressed up as women to act as decoys), voluntary 'vigilante' patrols, bloodhounds and journalists all searched for him in that small area, but he slipped past every time in spite of bloodstains on his clothes.

On one occasion, the night of a double murder (30th September), it is probable that he was hiding in the yard where he had murdered a woman when a hawker drove in with his pony and trap and the animal shied at the smell of fresh blood. The hawker jumped down to see what was wrong and discovered the corpse of Elizabeth Stride, blood still pouring from her throat. As he knelt beside her, the Ripper slipped away and vanished.

## Real Horrors

There have been other murderers who were never caught (like 'Jack the Stripper', who killed six women in 1964), but they never caused the same sensation. One reason for his exceptional notoriety is the flourish with which he signed himself when he wrote his macabre letters to the newspapers:

> 'How can they catch me now? I love my work and want to start again. You will soon hear of me and my funny little games.
>
> I saved some of the proper red stuff in a ginger beer bottle over the last job, to write with, but it went thick like glue and I can't use it. Red ink is fit enough I hope. Ha! Ha!
>
> The next job I do I shall clip the lady's ears off and send to the police officers just for jolly wouldn't you. Keep this letter back till I do a bit more work, then give it out straight.
>
> My knife is nice and sharp I want to get to work right away if I get a chance. Good luck.
>
> Yours truly,
> Jack the Ripper.'

Jack the Ripper – it was the perfect name! Alarming, memorable and deadly accurate, as police photographs of the victims prove.

But why did he cause such panic in 1888, when the East End was a sprawling, festering port, a melting-pot of nationalities where the cry of 'murder' was so common that people took no notice? Partly because murder *was* commonplace. The Ripper shone a spotlight on the dreadful conditions and poverty which people preferred to ignore, pretending they did not exist. He put an end to such pretence and shocked the conscience of the 'upper-classes'. Queen Victoria demanded an investigation and insisted on better street-lighting and clergymen thundered out sermons from their pulpits. An American actor, Richard Mansfield, even withdrew his production at the Lyceum of *Dr Jekyll and Mr Hyde* because, as the *Daily Telegraph* put it, 'There is quite sufficient to make us shudder out of doors.' Ironically, Jack the Ripper was the greatest reformer the East End knew. Conditions were never so bad again.

But why did he kill? What was the nature of the murders? Was there a pattern? a motive? It seemed that the victims were chosen at random, and this was a terrifying thought, for it meant that no one was safe. Certainly he did not kill for money. Apart from his last victim, Mary Kelly, they were pathetic, middle-aged women who had come down in the world and stayed in dismal doss-houses if they could afford the few pennies to do so.

But Mary Kelly was different – she was younger, prettier, and lived in a rented room of her own. It was noticed that the Ripper's murders grew more ferocious every time, as if they were building up to a climax. The murder of Kelly could hardly have been more horrible. He cut her up into such small pieces that the room afterwards resembled a butcher's shop. It took hours to reassemble the body and bloodstains marked the walls for years afterwards. There was so much blood that it seems probable that the Ripper was naked as he practised his butchery, slipping out at dawn to mingle with the crowds that were starting to flock merrily towards the Lord Mayor's Show.

A photographer took a close-up of Mary Kelly's eyes in the belief that the last image remains on the retina. This theory is described, horribly but brilliantly, in Rudyard Kipling's short story *At the End of the Passage*. Of course, nothing at all was found. This was the end for the Commissioner of Police, Sir Charles Warren, whose resignation was greeted with cheers in the House of Commons. It was the end for the Ripper too. Either he had been searching for Mary Kelly in particular, had found her and had taken his revenge, or his blood-lust had worn itself out and he could go no further.

Who was Jack the Ripper? This is another reason why his name lives on – Hunt the Ripper has become a national game in Britain. At first people imagined the Ripper to be a wild, black-bearded foreigner with a bagful of sharpened knives. Other suggestions include 'a Jewish slaughterman', 'A Tsarist political agent', an eminent doctor, a midwife (Jill the Ripper), a mad poet, and – most colourful of all – the Duke of Clarence, heir to the British throne who died soon after the murders and was succeeded by his brother who became King George V. There is no evidence to prove any man guilty.

Perhaps the closest we shall ever get is the evidence discovered by the author of this book, who has written about it previously (*Jack the Ripper* by Daniel Farson). I was staying with a friend in the North of Wales in 1959, and mentioned that I was preparing a television programme on the Ripper. Learning this, my hostess remarked: 'That's an extraordinary coincidence: my mother-in-law knows a lot about it, and we're seeing her this afternoon.' The Dowager Lady Aberconway, who died in 1975, was the daughter of Sir Melville Macnaghten. He was in charge of Scotland Yard after the murders and was responsible for completing the Ripper file. After his death, Lady Aberconway copied out his private notes and gave these to me, and in this way I learnt, for the first time, the name of the man the police suspected.

Montague John Druitt was an unsuccessful barrister and schoolmaster, dismissed from his school at Blackheath in that autumn of 1888. He was not a doctor, as Macnaghten believed, but his father, uncle and cousin were all doctors. At one time his cousin had a surgery in the Minories – right in the Ripper district, no more than a minute's walk from Mitre Square where Catherine Eddowes was killed in the double murder of 30th September. Educated at Winchester and Oxford, he was an ace cricketer.

But why consider him guilty? Because he fits the pattern. He drowned himself in the Thames after the last murder, and this certainly fits the theory that the Ripper could go no further. There is evidence that he was suspected by his own brother, who informed the police, but they tried to 'hush it up' as far as possible. The 'vigilante' patrols were called off in 1889, with no reason given except that the Ripper had been found 'drowned in the Thames'. The great forensic expert and authority on the Ripper, the late Professor Francis Camps, was convinced of Druitt's guilt: 'I am sure this is the answer at last.'

Was Druitt mad? In Sir Melville Macnaghten's words: '... after his awful glut [in Miller's Court, where Kelly lived] his brain gave way altogether.' It is possible that the opposite happened, and that as he walked into the void of dawn, his brain trembled for a moment and he realised what he had done. He revealed this in papers left for his brother William, and then took his own appalled and appalling life.

There is no absolute proof, and there probably never will be any, but it appears that M. J. Druitt is the person most likely to have been Jack the Ripper.

## The Vampire killer

All murder is horrible though some murderers are more horrible than others. The only reason for singling out John George Haigh from this century is that some people believe he was a sort of vampire.

Basil Copper (in *The Vampire*) claims:

> 'Though it has long been a matter of dispute among medical circles, there is no doubt in my mind that John George Haigh was a vampire in the classical tradition, possibly the only true monster in this field in the twentieth century. By this, of course, I do not mean to imply that he was a vampire in the supernatural sense, but there is at least a strong suggestion that he needed to drink blood in order to refresh and sustain himself.'

When he was arrested in 1949, the *Daily Mirror* newspaper headlined a sensational story about a 'vampire killer', but he was better known as the 'acid bath murderer', for this was how he disposed of his victims. He liquidated, literally, nine people – or so he claimed.

Haigh's childhood was strict; his parents described themselves as 'God's elect' and even rebuked a schoolmaster who loaned the boy a copy of *Treasure Island*. In spite of, or because of, this upbringing, he started a life of petty fraud at an early age. When he was released from Lincoln Prison in the war, he was involved in a car crash:

> 'Blood poured from my head and down my face and into my mouth. This revived in me the taste [for blood] and that night I experienced another awful dream. I saw before me a forest of crucifixes, which

gradually turned into trees. At first there appeared to be dew, or rain dripping from the branches but as I approached I realised it was blood. Suddenly the whole forest began to writhe and the trees, stark and erect, to ooze blood. A man went up to each tree catching the blood. When the cup was full he approached me. "Drink" he said, but I was unable to move and the dream faded.'

This is an extraordinary parallel to *The Death of Halpin Frayser*, a short story by Ambrose Bierce (see Chapter 4).

Haigh claimed he tapped blood from the necks of his victims and drank it in a mug. Could this be true? It is difficult to drain blood after death, and drinking it must be literally sick-making. 'It was their blood I was after ... I drank the blood for three to five minutes ... and afterwards I felt better,' he claimed at his trial. His fantasies of blood could have been a deliberate lie in the hope of being found 'guilty but insane', but even if this was calculated, he was no more sane than Elizabeth Bathory, Jack the Ripper or even Vlad Tepes, who forced mothers to eat their own babies. Certainly he had no conscience. He referred to his arrest as 'this pickle', and looked forward to the trial ('it should be fun'). He boasted: 'It isn't everybody can create more sensation than a film star.'

John George Haigh, the 'vampire killer' and 'acid bath murderer', was hanged in August 1949. One of his last acts was to leave his best suit for a waxworks figure in London's 'house of wax', Madame Tussauds – most appropriate! The Chamber of Horrors is just where all these human monsters should be.

# ANSWERS TO THE HORROR QUIZ

1. Edinburgh
2. Lord Dufferin
3. Count Dracula
4. Lady Arabella March
5. Bela Lugosi
6. Edgar Allan Poe
7. He stabbed his 'double', which was himself
8. Robert Louis Stevenson – *The Strange Case of Dr Jekyll and Mr Hyde*
9. The fifth Earl of Caernarvon
10. Lon Chaney Snr
11. Dr Moreau
12. Bram Stoker
13. Garlic or a cross
14. Justine
15. It aged while he stayed young
16. Jack Pierce
17. Erik
18. Boris Karloff
19. Croglin Grange
20. Hyde

21  Yes – a white one
22  Harry Price
23  Borley Rectory
24  Yes
25  Haiti
26  Lake Geneva
27  Quasimodo
28  You're a werewolf!
29  Robert Louis Stevenson
30  Prince Vlad V of Wallachia

# POSTSCRIPT

*'The children have never
fallen for my nonsense!'*

(Boris Karloff)

# Acknowledgements

The publishers are grateful to the following for permission to reproduce illustrations:
Barnaby's Picture Library – 19; Camera Press – 18; Mrs Imogen Dennis (St Pancras Public Libraries) – 2; Mary Evans Picture Library – 23; Daniel Farson – 15 (Miracle Films) and 13; Alan Frank – 4 (RKO) and 14 (Hammer); The Mansell Collection – 1, 6, 7, 10, 17, 21 and 22; National Film Archive – 3, 11 and 16 (Universal Pictures Co.); 5 (RKO) and 9 (MGM).

# More Beaver Books

We hope you have enjoyed this Beaver Book. Here are some of the other titles:

**Ghostly and Ghastly** A Beaver original. Thirteen stories of ghostly happenings collected by Barbara Ireson and illustrated by William Geldart make a spine-chilling read for everyone from nine upwards

**Covens and Cauldrons** An anthology of stories, folk tales, poems and legends about witches, edited by Jacynth Hope-Simpson and strikingly illustrated by Krystyna Turska

**Storm Warning** A powerful novel for older readers set in pre-war Nazi Germany, about a young English girl who helps two Jewish children escape from the Gestapo. By Mara Kay

**The Beaver Book of Gadgets** Harvey Weiss gives easy-to-follow instructions for making all sorts of gadgets including lamps, mobiles, games and even a burglar alarm! Fully illustrated with line drawings, for the nimble-fingered of nine upwards

New Beavers are published every month, and if you would like the *Beaver Bulletin* – which gives all the details – please send a large stamped addressed envelope to:

**Beaver Bulletin**
The Hamlyn Group
Astronaut House
Feltham
Middlesex TW14 9AR